HEALTHY, My WAY

HEALTHY,
My WAY

Real Food, Real Flavor, Real Good

MY NGUYEN

RODALE

NEW YORK

Contents

Chapter 1

FLAVOR BOMBS

Chapter 2

THE BREAKFAST BUFFET

Chapter 3

SNACKY THINGS

Introduction

PEOPLE OFTEN ASSUME I GREW UP WITH a wooden spoon in my hand. After all, my parents owned and ran a Vietnamese restaurant for years and my brother is a professional chef; cooking must be in my DNA, right? In reality, nothing could be further from the truth. With two doting parents who showed their love by putting multicourse meals on the table every day, even when our finances were tight, and then later, having the restaurant as my own personal canteen, I really never had to cook, and frankly, I wasn't that interested. When I left for college, I could barely make a PB&J. Even after I married my husband, Harlan, dinner more often than not was fast food or a Hungry Man meal for him and a Lean Cuisine for me!

It wasn't until my twin daughters arrived that I realized I needed to start getting more serious about eating well, both to help me get back into shape after childbirth and, just as importantly, to start my girls off on a path to good health from the moment they started eating solid food. Plus, I knew I wouldn't be able to keep up with two active toddlers, a high-intensity job in the mortgage industry, and a bustling household if I wasn't fueling myself with high-quality nutrients that gave me energy and kept me strong.

Not only that, weight was starting to accumulate in a way that I wasn't loving. I couldn't just work off a weekend of pizza and burgers with an extra hour in the gym the way I once could, and honestly, I just didn't feel that great. I knew if I was going to right the ship and get on a path to better health and a weight that made me feel good about myself, it had to start with cooking. After all, it was not lack of exercise that was packing on the pounds, it was too much processed, prepared food. It was time to get in the kitchen and really understand what I was putting on the table and in my body.

With a little encouragement from my nightly Food Network fix (a shout-out to my girl Rachael Ray!), I slowly began to get more comfortable as a cook, quickly progressing from basic staples like tuna salad and baked chicken to more involved dishes. When I started experimenting, I realized that I didn't need to follow every recipe to the letter and that I could play with flavors and ingredients to make things taste the way *I* liked them, and that made me feel good.

Since one of my goals was keeping my weight in check, my menus reflected whatever guidelines the diet du jour recommended, and I ping-ponged from keto to no-carb to high-protein and back again. But after a few months of forcing myself to follow restrictive diets and packing my plate with the kind of food we generally think of as healthy—so much quinoa, soooo many kale salads—I had to face facts: No way could I eat like this forever. It was food, and it certainly provided fuel, but was it exciting to eat? Did I look forward to mealtime? Not really. (Don't tell anyone, but I actually don't love quinoa. Does anyone?) Even worse, because my meals were so unsatisfying, I was losing the battle with between-meal snacking and eating way too many desserts.

Plus, my days were just too full to spend extra time making a health-conscious meal for myself and another for my husband, kids, and parents, who lived with me at the time. Let's face it, no matter how many dried cranberries or croutons you add, it's just about impossible to get a toddler to eat a kale salad!

My big breakthrough came when I realized that flavor had to come first; it couldn't just be all about getting the right number of macros in. If you're happy subsisting on an endless loop of grilled chicken breasts with steamed veggies on the side, good for you—that makes things easy. But I need a lot more color, crunch, and variety in my meals to keep me excited, and I know I'm not the only one.

I stopped counting calories and grams of this or that and started to define my *own* kind of healthy eating, one that minimized carbs, fats, and processed sugar in a low-key way while maximizing flavor and plate appeal. Instead of building my meals around a carb like rice, noodles, or pasta (not exactly intuitive for someone raised to believe a big bag of rice is the perfect housewarming gift!), I doubled down on lean proteins, vegetables, and

ingredients like fresh herbs and condiments that boosted flavors even further. Whenever I could, I made the cooking process more streamlined, cutting time (and fat) with my trusty air fryer and my own pragmatic kitchen hacks. And I cut way back on the amount of dairy and wheat I was eating.

The changes felt subtle and *manageable,* and before long I was back to a weight I felt good about. Better yet, I was cooking and eating food my family and I genuinely looked forward to, and none of us ever felt like we were on a diet.

And that's how @MyHealthyDish came into being. What started as a way to document some of my more successful kitchen forays and share the food of my Vietnamese heritage with what I assumed would be a tiny audience of family and friends soon became a full-time occupation—lucky for me, since I'd had to move in with my parents again after the mortgage industry tanked. Today I am a full-time content creator, and together with a few million of my closest friends, I'm continuing to grow as a cook and expanding my horizons with new ingredients and flavors every single day.

As the product of a California upbringing, I gravitate toward food that looks and tastes fresh, an eclectic mix of influences and cuisines that puts great produce and lean proteins at the center of the plate. I aim for meals that are nutrient-dense, meaning no calories are wasted on empty carbs and other fillers that do nothing to keep me strong and healthy. And I continue to keep an eye on sugar and avoid too much salt, two "nutrients" none of us needs more of. The result is food that keeps me satisfied, nourishes my body without weighing it down, and is full of addictively delicious colors, flavors, and textures.

Many of the recipes in this book take their inspiration from my Southeast Asian heritage as well as the cuisines of China, Korea, or Japan, not just because I love those flavors and ingredients, but because they are naturally gluten- and

dairy-free. With simple modifications, like swapping out some of the carbs for more veggies (I am *always* pushing myself to eat more veggies) and including a bit more protein than is traditional on an Asian table, these recipes work with just about any kind of healthy meal plan.

But with a husband who grew up on a pretty standard meat-and-potatoes diet and two teens who eat like teenagers do, I make sure to cater to their tastebuds too. From an easy Chili Beef Skillet Dinner (page 179) to a dairy-free Creamy Roasted Tomato Soup (page 116), an irresistible layered dip with Greek salad vibes (page 93), and my take on street tacos (page 185), there is something here to make everyone at my table (and yours!) happy. Once picky eaters who longed for McDonald's, my

girls now prefer my cooking to what we get at restaurants, and I'm making sure that they get plenty of time to play in the kitchen too, starting them off on a path to lifelong good health a lot sooner than I did!

In the pages that follow, I will lay out my key strategies for keeping it light without losing out on taste or compulsively counting calories. (Spoiler: Upending your carb-to-veggie ratio is an important first step.) I'll explain how I use some ingredients commonly associated with Southeast Asian cooking in unexpected new ways to make food with a bright kick and plenty of plate appeal. And I'll show you how to stock your fridge and pantry so you're never more than a few minutes away from a meal that looks as good as it tastes.

HOW I DO
"Healthy"

When I was deciding what to name this cookbook, I wondered if people would take issue with the title of being healthy *my* way. After all, we all know what's healthy and what isn't, right? Well, not necessarily. The thing I've come to understand about the word *healthy* is that it's a moving target, something that changes as science learns more about how we use nutrients—and as my body and its needs change. What medical experts consider to be a "healthy" diet has changed a lot in the last twenty-five years.

More important, what I *personally* consider healthy has evolved, too. As a woman going through different hormonal stages of life, I find what once worked for me no longer does. When I was in my twenties and thirties, it was mainly about staying thin. If I noticed a few extra pounds creeping up on me, all I had to do was hit the gym for a couple of extra hours and skip a lunch or two, and bingo, I was back in my size 6 jeans. Now that I am in my forties, I still keep an eye on the scale, but I'm just as concerned with feeling energetic, avoiding that uncomfortable, bloated feeling, and sleeping well. I also don't want to submit my body to the stress of blood sugar spikes and drops. Eating well *nearly* all of the time helps me achieve all that and more.

There are many diets out there, and I bet you have tried a few of them. Paleo, keto, vegan, raw food—all of these have had their moment in the sun and honestly, if dropping a few pounds in a hurry is your goal, any of them will probably help you do just that . . . for a while. But here's the thing: Any diet that involves restrictions or deprivation becomes unsustainable over time. And when you are told you *can't* eat something, eventually it will become the *only* thing you want to eat, right? I know that's how it works for me! That's why my definition of *healthy* includes *all* the foods I crave, even chocolate.

But while I don't eliminate anything from my diet completely, I do try to limit my carbs, because I am not as active as I once was, so my body doesn't need as much quick-access energy. I find I am at my best when I increase my protein and veggies, keep portion sizes in check, and eat real food, meaning food that I make from scratch using unprocessed ingredients that my body can metabolize steadily and slowly. It's what works for me and I'm guessing many women in their thirties, forties, and beyond can benefit from it as well. Even though I'm spending much less time at the gym these days, I find the approach helps me maintain a weight and energy level I am happy with. I still enjoy a burger or pizza now and then, but as long as I am eating healthy *my* way most of the time, I don't need to beat myself up if I stray off the straight and narrow occasionally.

Eating this way was hardly second nature to me. I was a toddler when my family first came to this country, and we didn't have many resources. Frankly, money was tight most of the time. My brothers and I grew up eating fast food, Spam, and government cheese. Meat was an infrequent luxury,

and whatever fish or protein we did have was always extended with plenty of inexpensive starches and vegetables. To this day, I'm always fighting the pull of the processed food I was weaned on, and if I'm being totally honest, Spam and rice with a side of crackers and block cheese is still my happy place. I had to educate myself—and my palate—to appreciate not only the way real food tastes, but also how it makes me feel afterward.

Over time I've come to realize that the way I cook, combining my Vietnamese heritage with a Cali-fresh twist, hits all the right notes when it comes to clean, nutrient-dense, and delicious eating. I love to take a traditional dish like banh mi or fried rice and double or even triple the amount of herbs and veggies you'd find in most recipes, while dialing back the amount of rice, noodles, and other carb-y elements. I've also adapted dishes that might have been fried to work in the oven or the air fryer and replaced high-fat proteins with leaner, cleaner alternatives. At this point, these swaps are second nature to me, and after you have used my recipes for a while, they will be for you, too.

Time and time again, it's been proven that the best diet is one that encompasses a broad range of *real* (not processed or packaged) foods with an emphasis on vegetables, lean proteins, and a moderate amount of grains and other carbs. That's the not-so-secret secret to eating healthy, my way, and it informs every recipe in this book. Here's what that looks like in my kitchen:

BE CONSCIOUS (BUT NOT FRIGHTENED) OF CARBS

Nutritional and medical experts don't agree on much, but one thing that no one seems to dispute is that we all get far more carbohydrates than we need strictly for fuel, especially simple carbs like sugar and highly processed grains. For that reason, carbs in most forms, whether as a grain like bread or pasta, or in the form of sugar, are the one nutrient I am most strict about. No one who grew up in an Asian household could eliminate rice from their diet entirely, but many of my recipes extend the carb component with another ingredient— usually a vegetable—so there are fewer carbs and more veggies in every mouthful. Fill your spring rolls with some blanched bean sprouts instead of vermicelli noodles, as I did in the spring rolls on page 94. I lighten up my Furikake Potato Salad (page 192) by swapping in chunks of cooked cauliflower for half of the potatoes, and because they have a similar texture, no one is ever the wiser.

My Golden Rules

1. Minimize (but don't eliminate) carbs.
2. Maximize vegetables—have some at every meal if you can!
3. Go easy on dairy.
4. Go hard on fresh herbs, citrus, and other natural flavor enhancers.
5. Enjoy red meat as an occasional treat.
6. Give refined sugar a miss whenever possible—but don't take all the sweetness out of life!

DOUBLE DOWN ON VEGGIES

Why use one vegetable when you can use two or more? I like a mix of textures and flavors in my meals, and using a combination of vegetables is an easy way to achieve that while upping the nutritional value of your food. It's almost impossible to overdo veggies, so don't hold back! If a recipe calls for spinach, add some arugula or chard, or add some thawed edamame to your salads and stir-fries, even if they're not on the ingredient list. I sneak broccoli into so many things, from noodle soups to tuna salad. And I put avocado—not too much; even good fat is still fat—into just about everything. Zucchini is another vegetable that can be grated into meatballs or tortillas, or added to cooked and raw dishes; so is fennel.

Measure for Measure

If you have watched me cook, you know that precise measurements are not exactly my thing. Since this is a cookbook, I have included quantities to guide you, but you should always cook to please your own palate and adjust the flavors to your liking. An extra teaspoon of soy sauce or fish sauce here, a little less garlic or sugar there, an extra squirt of lime juice or handful of scallions will not affect the outcome of the recipe other than to make it even more delightful to your tastebuds! You may also notice that I have not been super specific about sizes when it comes to vegetables because I never want you feel that you have to make a grocery run to get a large sweet potato if you only have a medium one in order to make dinner. If I call for an onion, whatever size you have will be just fine—even that half onion nearly forgotten in your crisper. If you like carrots, use a big one; if not, use a small one or leave it out altogether. That's what I do, and I never hear a complaint about a dish being short an ounce or two of onions! Remember, it's just cooking, and it should be fun!

PROTEIN POWER

Whenever possible, I prefer to beef up the protein content of my recipes, no pun intended. In Vietnamese cooking, meat is generally served as a condiment; without changing the overall flavor profile, I like to flip that ratio so that meat and vegetables take center stage while the starchy accompaniment becomes a bit player. Sometimes that simply means adding a little more meat, poultry, or seafood to a dish than would traditionally be included, but at other times, I use one of the options below instead of meat to add creamy body and substance as well as a few extra grams of protein:

TOFU

When I am making a meatless meal, I rely on firm or extra-firm tofu as a primary protein source in soups, stir-fries, and even dumplings. But my real ace in the hole is soft or silken tofu. Its smooth, creamy texture makes it the perfect way to add protein to puddings, egg dishes, and even smoothies, and its flavor is so mild that you won't even know it's there.

BEANS AND LEGUMES

Many of the soups and salads in this book make use of canned beans, as they are inexpensive, taste great, and are also a good source of fiber and other beneficial nutrients.

COTTAGE CHEESE AND GREEK YOGURT

I am a new convert to cottage cheese, which is actually higher in protein than yogurt. For years, its lumpy, curd-like consistency relegated it to a 1950s-style diet plate, but once it is whipped in a blender or food processor, the texture becomes downright dreamy. I spread it on my breakfast toast, stir it into parfaits and chia puddings, and use it to give my artichoke dip a creamy texture. Greek yogurt, although higher in fat than cottage cheese, has a delicious tang that I think works particularly well with fruit in desserts and breakfast bowls.

PEANUT BUTTER POWDER

I love the flavor of peanut butter, and with peanut butter powder, you get all of the taste and protein with virtually none of the fat. It's also a good binder in things like my Chewy Chocolate Nut Bars on page 88, and it can be stirred into yogurt for a quick, tasty snack. You'll find it in most well-stocked grocery stores near the peanut butter. It's on the pricey side, but it is quite versatile, and a couple of tablespoons will go a long way.

My high-protein, low-fat lox spread is made with cottage cheese; rich chocolate mousse, opposite, has a base of silken tofu.

TEMPT WITH TEXTURE

When you are trying to make interesting, craveable food without a lot of unwanted fats, calories, or carbs, texture is your secret weapon. In Vietnamese cooking, a sprinkle of fried shallots, a pile of pickled vegetables, or the snap of sliced cucumber is the finishing touch to so many dishes, and I apply that philosophy to almost every dish I serve, whatever its roots. Our brains are highly attuned to textures in our food and it's as much a part of what makes food enjoyable as the flavors themselves. Just think about how much more appealing a french fry is when it's crispy-crunchy than limp and soggy! The same holds true for everything from salads and soups to your breakfast parfaits. When a dish contains a mixture of crunchy, creamy, firm, or soft textures, it excites your palate, and your brain experiences pleasure—even when no actual cream or frying are involved!

ADD SOME ACID, HEAT, AND A FRESH NOTE

To someone raised on Vietnamese food, reaching for a wedge of lime and a squirt of sriracha when someone puts a bowl of pho in front of me is second nature, as instinctive as grabbing a bottle of ketchup when a burger arrives. You'll notice many of these recipes get brightness from a dash of citrus or vinegar, as well as chiles, whether they're fresh or in the form of dried flakes, infused chili garlic oil, or hot sauce. Lastly, I always like to add a fresh element with a handful of fresh herbs or a few crisp, leafy greens. Adding these extra notes keeps my dishes from tasting (and looking!) flat and one-dimensional.

What If You Have Special Dietary Needs?

I don't have an issue with gluten, but many people do, and where there is gluten there are usually carbs galore, so gluten is not something you will encounter very often in this book. Because wheat is not widely cultivated in Asia, rice is the starch of choice for those of us who grew up eating and cooking Asian food, either as a cooked grain or in the form of noodles, spring roll wrappers, or flour. For that reason, with just a few exceptions, you will be able to cook very easily from the recipes in this book if you or a family member have a sensitivity to gluten. In those few instances where I do call for ingredients that contain gluten, such as pasta, bread, or all-purpose flour, you can easily substitute your favorite gluten-free stand-in.

Dairy is a bit trickier. Dairy products are hard for many people to digest (including those whose genetic heritage, like mine, leads to Asia or Africa), and they are also connected with inflammatory responses in the body. Who needs that? While I don't avoid dairy absolutely, I limit my consumption mostly to options that provide plenty of protein, like cottage cheese and Greek yogurt, and am careful about how often I eat them. In most cases, the recipes in this book can be made with an equivalent plant-based product, like coconut yogurt or almond milk, a tactic I encourage you to employ if you prefer to limit dairy's presence in your diet.

STOCKING MY HEALTHY KITCHEN
(and yours)

It is a truism that cooking starts at the grocery store; you simply can't make good meals from subpar ingredients. I don't mean that you need to shop exclusively at high-end stores or go 100 percent organic, although if that's your preference and it fits your budget, by all means, go for it. But wherever you shop, there are better choices to be made, and it all comes down to focusing on real food and clean ingredients that are as unprocessed as possible.

With just a few exceptions, you will be able to find the ingredients I rely on in any well-stocked grocery store. Ingredients that once upon a time might have been considered exotic, like fish sauce, Korean gochujang, za'atar, and different varieties of rice and noodles, are now widely available in almost any grocery store, as are bok choy, fresh lemongrass, and bean sprouts. That said, if you happen to have an Asian grocery near you, it's well worth making an outing there to save time, money, and frustration. (See "Since You Made the Trip . . ." on page 23.)

As you page through this book you'll see that many of my recipes draw from Asian culinary traditions, including my own Vietnamese heritage as well as Chinese, Korean, and Japanese cooking. Here are the ingredients you'll want to have in your pantry:

Soy sauce: The basic flavoring ingredient common to most Asian cooking.

Fish sauce: This pungent condiment made from fermented fish is used throughout Southeast Asia and adds salty, savory notes to soups, sauces, and dips.

Hoisin sauce: A little bit salty, a little bit sweet, this thick, dark brown sauce adds body and depth to marinades, stir fries, and more.

Oyster sauce: Less sweet than hoisin sauce, oyster sauce is another thick, flavorful, super-savory condiment that is especially good with veggies.

Sesame oil: Sesame oil is highly fragrant and potently flavored, and for that reason is used sparingly, often as a finishing touch or in raw dishes like salads. Look for a deep golden toasted sesame oil, not a pale, wheat-colored oil meant for cooking.

Rice vinegar: Rice vinegar has a mild flavor and relatively low acidity that makes it perfect for seasoning sushi rice and salad dressings.

Sriracha: No doubt you already have this mildly spicy, garlic-enhanced hot sauce on your shelf; I wouldn't eat a bowl of pho without a hefty squirt!

Black vinegar: Essential for dumpling sauce, black vinegar has a deeper, more aged flavor than rice vinegar and is less sweet than balsamic.

Dark soy sauce: Although it is thicker and more intense than regular soy, dark soy is primarily used to add color to a dish rather than flavor. If you don't have it, you can just omit it from your recipe.

Kewpie mayonnaise: A Japanese product that is thinner and tangier than standard mayo and comes in a handy squeeze bottle.

Sesame seeds: You'll want these for salads, furikake, and dressings. Having both black and white seeds is nice for variety and makes an appealing garnish.

Gochugaru: This gently spicy Korean ground red pepper powder can be used wherever you want a bit of subtle heat.

Chinese five-spice powder: An aromatic blend of ground spices that includes star anise, cinnamon, and pepper; I especially like it with chicken and squash.

Pho seasoning and spice bags: I buy a pre-blended mix of whole black cardamom and coriander seeds, star anise pods, cloves, and cinnamon sticks. If your store doesn't carry pho spices, you can buy the individual spices and make your own mix (page 28).

Mushroom bouillon powder: Just a teaspoon adds incredible depth and umami flavor to broths, soups, sauces, and even kale chips. Once you've used this ingredient a few times, I guarantee it will make its way into lots of recipes in your repertoire for an instant flavor upgrade.

Tamarind paste: You can buy tamarind in the form of concentrate, whole pods, extract, and powder. I prefer the paste, which comes in pliable blocks, but any form will give the puckery tang you want from this tropical fruit; you may just need to adjust the amount used.

Rock sugar: I use this almost exclusively in pho, but you can substitute Demerara or brown sugar in a pinch.

Noodles: Fresh, vacuum-packed rice noodles for pho, glass (yam) noodles, rice vermicelli, and soba noodles are the varieties I call for in this book.

Rice-paper rounds and wonton wrappers: These are for dumplings, spring rolls, and more.

Thai basil: A uniquely fragrant and delicious herb that is absolutely required for a good bowl of pho, Thai basil has deep purple stems and smaller pointed leaves than its Italian counterpart. If you can't find a reliable source nearby, consider growing your own. Either way, seek it out—you won't be sorry.

All of these ingredients appear in this book's recipes, and you'll avoid frustration if you add them to your shopping list before you get down to cooking. You may not need to make a special trip to find them, but more than likely, you'll be able to buy them more inexpensively and find a wider selection to choose from, at an Asian market. And check out the list opposite for other items you'll want to add to your shopping list.

Waste Not, Want Not

Like many people who grew up without much money, I consider myself a frugal cook who hates the idea of wasting food. I won't ask you to buy ingredients you'll use once and push to the back of your fridge or pantry, or leave you with an open can of beans or a half block of tofu. Look for this ✽ symbol to point you toward other recipes that will help you use up that can, bottle, or jar, so nothing goes down the drain or in the trash.

SINCE YOU MADE THE TRIP . . .

I may be biased here, but for my money, there are certain items I *could* get at my regular supermarket but prefer to buy at an Asian market when I'm doing a pantry refresh because the selection is superior and the prices are lower—sometimes *much* lower. Once you get past the variety of choices (which can be overwhelming for newbies), you'll quickly see there are a hundred and one reasons to do at least part of your shopping at an Asian market, whether or not any Asian meals are on your horizon. Here is my far-from-complete list of what to zero in on:

Spices: Not only Asian spices but also cinnamon, cumin, ginger, and many more are sold in generous quantities for a fraction of what you'll spend on a small glass jar of them at your grocery store.

Fresh mushrooms: Look for shiitakes, enoki, king oyster, maitakes, and more, all gently priced.

Rice, noodles, and ramen: You may not need to buy your rice twenty pounds at a time like I do, but why not get an economy-sized bag and buy yourself peace of mind that you won't run out any time soon? And if you are going to eat packaged ramen, at least go for the good stuff, not the five-for-a-dollar bargain brands—the flavors are so much better. Stroll down the noodle aisle and pick out one or two types to experiment with, whether they're fresh, frozen, or dried; made from buckwheat, yam starch, tofu, or green tea; or are any of the hundred other varieties. None of them will break the bank, so what do you have to lose? You may discover a new favorite.

Green veggies: Broaden your vegetable horizons with water spinach, gai lan, pea shoots, flowering cauliflower, and baby bok choy, just for starters (see pages 198 and 203 for tips on cooking them). I also use a ton of scallions, and buy them here three or four bunches at a time.

Fruit: In my opinion, the fruit I get at the Asian market is sweeter and of better quality than what I see at the supermarket, whether it's the Fuji apples I craved when I was pregnant, or fresh citrus and pineapples. Look for interesting fruits that rarely make it to the ShopRite, like jackfruit, dragon fruit, and pomelos.

Fresh herbs: Beyond the Thai basil mentioned earlier (facing page), look for reasonably priced packages of mint, cilantro, dill, and scallions.

Aromatics: Ginger, fresh turmeric, shallots, and lemongrass will be fresher and more affordable here than elsewhere because the turnover is so much higher. I also buy peeled garlic by the quart container, and it is a real time-saver.

Chapter 1

FLAVOR BOMBS

My Essential Sauces, Seasonings, and Flavor Boosters

IN MOST COOKBOOKS, YOU WOULD PROBABLY FIND this chapter hidden at the back of the book, almost an afterthought. I've chosen to put it right up front because, for many of my recipes, this is where the flavor starts: a dressing, marinade, condiment, or sauce that wakes up simple ingredients.

I can hear you thinking, "Who has time to make this stuff from scratch—can't I just pick them up at the store?" Sure you can, if you like to pay a lot more and get a bunch of extra stuff like stabilizers, preservatives, too much salt, and hidden sugars. But I think you'll quickly come to see that getting a jump on weeknight meals by preparing some of these key building blocks in advance actually saves you a *ton* of time when you need to get dinner on the table. It's a small investment with a big payoff.

The handful of recipes I've chosen for this chapter are especially versatile and can be used to give just about anything you cook a swift kick of concentrated flavor. They are all simple enough to make as needed, but if you've had the foresight to prepare some Tamarind Ketchup (page 36) or Thai Basil Pesto (page 43) ahead of time (or made a double batch so you have extra for future meals), you'll find weeknight meals come together *so* much faster.

If you're someone who is always looking for ways to make leftovers seem like a brand-new meal, look no further. With a shake of DIY Furikake (page 32) or a drizzle of Avocado Sauce (page 42), yesterday's rotisserie chicken or grilled salmon becomes a fabulous sushi bake or the base of a grain bowl or a wrap sandwich. Even more importantly, they will taste like you spent a lot more time on prep than you actually did.

PHO SPICE SACHETS

Makes enough for 8 batches of pho

If you have access to a store that carries Vietnamese ingredients, you will likely be able to find packages of pre-mixed spices for flavoring your pho broth; otherwise, it is far, far better to make your own spice blend than to buy powdered "pho base" for your soup-making adventures. If you are ordering online, why not add a package of muslin spice bags to your cart, too? They aren't expensive and they are a lot easy to wrangle than the cheesecloth.

16 star anise pods
16 teaspoons coriander seeds
8 teaspoons whole cloves
8 teaspoons fennel seeds
24 black cardamom pods
8 2-inch pieces cinnamon
   stick

Arrange eight 6 × 6-inch pieces of cheesecloth on a work surface. Place 2 star anise pods, 2 teaspoons of coriander seeds, 1 teaspoon of cloves, 1 teaspoon of fennel seeds, 3 cardamom pods, and a piece of cinnamon stick in the center of each. Gather the cheesecloth into a pouch and tie with kitchen string.

Place the sachets in a freezer bag and press out all the air. Seal the bag and store in the freezer until ready to use.

28

MY SPICE BLEND

Makes about ¾ cup

It took writing a cookbook for me to realize how much time I spent measuring out half teaspoons of these basic spices, day in and day out. Now I just stir together a big batch of this all-purpose mixture and keep it stove-side to season meats, roasted vegetables, tofu, and stir-fries. Easy-peasy!

¼ cup kosher salt
2 tablespoons garlic powder
1 tablespoon onion powder
1 teaspoon smoked or regular paprika
¼ teaspoon Chinese five-spice powder

Combine the salt, garlic and onion powders, paprika, and five-spice powder in a small bowl and whisk them together until the spice blend is uniformly colored. Transfer to a small jar and store indefinitely at room temperature.

SOLID-GOLD TURMERIC PASTE

Makes about 1 cup

This versatile paste was inspired by jamu, an Indonesian juice drink made from ginger, turmeric, and coconut water. I've added a little bit of honey to tame the flames (raw ginger has a real bite) and lots of lemon. A tablespoon of this sunny blend mixed with any hot or cold liquid (even chicken broth, page 115!) is both warming and soothing at the same time and full of inflammation-fighting ingredients. Unlike its inspiration, the concentrated paste doesn't require a juicer, and it can be stored in the fridge or freezer to use whenever you feel a sniffle coming on. Fresh turmeric is readily available in most Asian markets (and a lot less expensive than it is at the natural foods store, too).

2 small lemons
3 ounces fresh ginger, peeled and coarsely chopped
4½ ounces fresh turmeric, peeled and coarsely chopped
3 tablespoons honey
½ teaspoon ground black pepper

With a sharp knife, slice the peel and pith from the lemons. Slice the flesh into chunks and discard as many seeds as possible.

Place the lemons in a food processor along with the ginger and turmeric and process to a paste. Add the honey and pepper and process again until combined.

Scrape the paste into a jar, cover, and refrigerate until ready to use or up to 1 week. For longer storage, scoop 1-tablespoon balls onto a parchment paper–lined baking sheet and freeze until solid. Store the frozen balls in a zip-top plastic bag for up to 6 months.

LEMONGRASS SHALLOT PASTE

Makes about ½ cup

You should be able to find fresh lemongrass in most well-stocked grocery stores, but to be honest, the tough stalks are kind of a pain to work with, requiring a very sharp knife and plenty of elbow grease to mince finely. You can take the easy route and buy prepared paste (usually found in the produce section), or do as I do and make your own much more delicious lemongrass paste for seasoning everything from pork and chicken for spring rolls and banh mi to a soothing mug of chicken broth. Pick the youngest, freshest lemongrass you can find and prep it right after you buy it, as lemongrass tends to dry out quickly. This does require a powerful blender or food processor; that blender you bought for making margaritas probably won't get the job done.

5 or 6 fresh lemongrass stalks
2 shallots, peeled and cut into chunks
4 garlic cloves
½ teaspoon kosher salt

Using a very sharp knife, trim off the tops and bottom inch of the lemongrass stalks, then peel and discard the outer two layers; the remaining stalk should be tender enough to slice fairly easily. Cut the lemongrass into ¼-inch pieces and place in a food processor along with the shallots, garlic, and salt. Pulse on and off a few times until the mixture is very finely minced. With the machine running, gradually add ¼ cup of water and continue to puree until the mixture forms a smooth, homogeneous paste. If it's still chunky and stringy-looking, continue to add water 1 teaspoon at a time. Transfer the mixture to a small jar and refrigerate to use within 3 or 4 days, or freeze in 1-tablespoon portions and store in a plastic bag in the freezer for up to 3 months.

DIY FURIKAKE

Makes a scant ½ cup

Think of this as the Asian forefather of everything bagel seasoning, a savory sprinkle that perks up anything from a plain bowl of rice to noodle soups, salads, steamed veggies—even popcorn. The nonnegotiable ingredients are nutty sesame seeds and shreds of dried seaweed, but bonito flakes are often added, for an earthy depth of flavor, as well as a pinch of salt (or sugar). I like to include dulse, another kind of dried seaweed with a mild, smoky flavor, but if you can't find it, just skip it. Make a big batch, transfer it to a jar, and unleash a flurry of flavors onto your eggs, sushi bakes . . . you get the idea.

½ sheet toasted nori seaweed

2 tablespoons white sesame seeds

1 tablespoon black sesame seeds

1 tablespoon dulse flakes (optional)

½ teaspoon flaky sea salt

Using a very sharp, large knife, cut the nori into four equal pieces, stack them, and then slice them as thinly as possible. Cut the strips crosswise into ¼-inch pieces; they should look like confetti.

Transfer the nori bits to a dry skillet and add the white and black sesame seeds and the dulse flakes, if using. Toast over medium heat, stirring constantly, until the sesame seeds start popping, just a minute or two. Immediately transfer to a bowl. Stir in the salt and let cool. Store the furikake in an airtight container indefinitely.

FRIED SHALLOTS

Makes 1 cup

The hardest part of making these addictive crunchy morsels is peeling all those shallots. But, on the plus side, in addition to fried shallots, you will end up with deliciously flavored oil to use in salad dressings, stir-fries, and more. I make these with shallots from the Asian market because they are about half the price of the larger, more elongated variety, but either type will work. You want really uniform, thin slices, so if you have a mandoline, now is the time to dig it out, but be careful not to shave your fingertips!

8 ounces shallots, peeled
  and thinly sliced
  (about 2½ cups)

2 cups canola oil
Kosher salt

In a large frying pan over medium-high heat, heat the canola oil until it shimmers (about 325°F on an instant-read thermometer). When you drop a piece of shallot into the oil, it should instantly sizzle. Set a fine-mesh strainer over a heatproof bowl.

Carefully add a big handful of shallots to the pan—the oil will bubble furiously, so stand back! Add the rest of the shallots, stir well, and fry until most of the shallots have turned light golden brown, about 15 minutes. It's okay if a few are still pale. Stir whenever the shallots at the perimeter of the pan are getting darker than those in the center.

Empty the pan into the strainer, reserving the oil. Using tongs, transfer the fried shallots to a paper-towel-lined plate to drain. Sprinkle with a few pinches of salt. When the shallots and oil have completely cooled, transfer them to separate jars with tight-fitting lids and store at room temperature for up to several weeks.

PICKLED VEGGIES

Makes about 4 cups

If you've ever had a banh mi sandwich, you know how essential these puckery tidbits are to balancing the fatty richness of pâté and grilled meats. Pickled vegetables are a great way to add crunch, color, and a bit of piquant flavor to salads and sandwiches, and you will always find them served alongside any kind of grilled meat or seafood in a Vietnamese spread. They are beyond simple to make and best of all, they are ready to eat in about an hour. Keep a jar in the fridge and you'll be surprised how often you find yourself reaching for it!

2 large carrots, peeled
1 small daikon radish, peeled
¾ cup distilled white vinegar
¼ cup sugar
1½ teaspoons kosher salt

Use a mandoline to julienne the carrots and radish or, with a sharp knife, cut them into fine 3-inch-long matchsticks. Place the carrots and daikon in a 1-quart jar with a lid or four 8-ounce jars.

In a large saucepan, combine the vinegar, sugar, salt, and 4 cups of water. Bring to a simmer over medium heat and stir until the sugar and salt are dissolved, about 1 minute. Carefully pour the hot liquid over the vegetables, filling the jar until the vegetables are completely submerged in the brine; you may not need it all. Let the pickled veggies cool to room temperature; they will be ready to eat in about an hour, but they can be refrigerated, covered, for up to 1 month. They'll taste a bit more tangy and pickled over time.

HOMEMADE SRIRACHA

Makes about 2 cups

When there was a global shortage of sriracha recently, some folks panicked; I got cooking! Turns out, the most difficult part of making this beloved hot sauce is waiting a full week for it to ferment, and all that requires is patience. It's so satisfying to see the bright-red final product, and the flavor is amazing!

1 pound red jalapeño peppers,
    stem ends removed

12 garlic cloves

3 tablespoons sugar

2 tablespoons kosher salt

¼ cup distilled white vinegar

Combine the jalapeños, garlic, sugar, and salt in a blender. Add ¼ cup water and blend until pureed.

Transfer the puree to a 1-quart glass jar and cover with a lid. Set in a cool, dark place for 7 days, or until bubbles are beginning to form in the jar, indicating fermentation is taking place.

Pour the fermented paste into a saucepan and add the vinegar. Bring to a simmer over medium heat and cook gently for 10 minutes, or until slightly thickened. Place a fine-mesh strainer over a bowl and use a rubber spatula to press the paste through the strainer. Discard the solids.

Transfer the sriracha to a clean jar or squeeze bottle and store in the refrigerator for up to 3 weeks.

TAMARIND KETCHUP

Makes about 2 cups

Sweet, sour, and slightly spicy, this bright, snappy sauce has so much more depth of flavor than your basic tomato ketchup but is just as versatile, and has a lot less sugar. Use it full strength as a dip for a shrimp cocktail, stir some into your favorite vinaigrette for a punchy salad dressing, or slather it on a turkey meat loaf. Yum!

4 ounces (about ½ cup)
    tamarind paste

½ cup boiling water

¼ cup maple syrup

2 tablespoons tomato paste

1 tablespoon Worcestershire
    sauce

2 teaspoons sriracha

1 teaspoon kosher salt

Juice of 2 limes

Break up the tamarind paste a bit with your fingers and place the chunks in a small bowl. Add the boiling water, cover with a plate, and set aside for 15 minutes to soften.

Using a rubber spatula, mash the tamarind paste into the soaking liquid until the puree is as smooth as possible. Place a mesh sieve over a medium bowl, pour in the puree, and press it through the sieve, discarding any solids. Whisk in the remaining ingredients and stir to combine well. Pour into a jar and seal with a tight-fitting lid. Store in the refrigerator for up to 1 month.

CHILI GARLIC OIL

Makes about ⅔ cup

Two kinds of dried chiles make this hot enough to burn your booty! The oil gives a lift to everything from steamed eggs to sushi bakes, and if you are a chili crisp fan, I bet you will find this equally addictive.

2 tablespoons minced garlic

1 large scallion (white and green parts), minced

1 tablespoon hot red pepper flakes

1 tablespoon gochugaru (Korean red pepper powder)

⅔ cup neutral oil, such as avocado or canola

In a medium heatproof bowl, combine the garlic, scallions, red pepper flakes, and gochugaru. In a small saucepan over medium-high heat, heat the oil until very hot. Immediately pour the hot oil over the garlic mixture and stir well to combine. When the oil is cool, transfer to a jar with a tight-fitting lid and store in the refrigerator for up to 2 weeks.

NUOC CHAM

Makes about ½ cup

This is the ubiquitous dresssing–dipping sauce you will find in most Vietnamese homes, and that I go through by the gallon in my own home. Every family makes theirs a bit differently, so it's no surprise that I like mine less sweet and a little spicier than some versions you may have tried, but feel free to tinker with the proportions. Add more water, sugar, or lime juice until it's just the way *you* like it!

2 garlic cloves, minced to a paste

2½ tablespoons fresh lime juice

2 tablespoons fish sauce

2 tablespoons sugar

1 red Thai chile, sliced or minced (optional)

In a small bowl or jar, mix together the garlic, lime juice, fish sauce, and 1 tablespoon of the sugar. Add ¼ cup of hot water and whisk or shake to combine. Give the sauce a taste and add the remaining 1 tablespoon of sugar if needed to balance the tart and savory flavors. Add the sliced chile, if using. The sauce can be refrigerated for up to 3 or 4 days.

THE VERY BEST DUMPLING SAUCE

Makes about ¾ cup

I consider this an all-purpose dipping sauce because it is just as tasty on your air-fried cauliflower bites as it is on homemade wontons or takeout dim sum. I wouldn't think of serving my Firecracker Salmon (page 100) without it, and it also makes a great marinade for meat, seafood, and even tofu. Without the fresh scallions and cilantro, it will keep just about indefinitely, so if you won't be using it all at once, just mix up the seasonings and add the greens when you're ready to use.

½ cup soy sauce

¼ cup toasted sesame oil

2 tablespoons black vinegar or rice vinegar

4 teaspoons brown sugar

1 tablespoon chili garlic oil, or to taste

2 tablespoons chopped scallions (green parts only)

2 tablespoons chopped fresh cilantro

In a small bowl, combine the soy sauce, sesame oil, vinegar, sugar, and chili garlic oil and whisk to combine. Stir in the scallions and cilantro and serve immediately. Store leftovers in a covered container and serve within 2 or 3 days for the best flavor.

AVOCADO SAUCE

Makes about 1¼ cups

My girls love this sauce on absolutely everything, from a breakfast burrito to fish, salads, and even Mexican entrées like the Chili Beef Skillet Dinner on page 179. The generous amount of cilantro ensures that the sauce stays bright green.

1 ripe avocado, peeled and pitted
½ cup lightly packed cilantro (including the tender stems)
½ cup reduced-fat sour cream
2 tablespoons fresh lime juice
½ teaspoon garlic powder
½ teaspoon kosher salt

In a blender, combine the avocado, cilantro, sour cream, lime juice, garlic powder, and salt and puree until smooth. If the sauce is too thick, add 1 tablespoon of water and mix again. Store the sauce in an airtight container in the refrigerator for up to 4 days.

THAI BASIL PESTO

Makes about 1 cup

Thai basil is an essential accompaniment to a bowl of pho, but that's just the beginning of the possibilities for this incredibly aromatic herb. I just can't get enough of its amazing, licorice-y fragrance and slightly spicy flavor. Like all varieties of basil, though, it doesn't have a long shelf life, so I often preserve any that I won't be using in the next day or two by whizzing up a quick pesto. This pesto is made with raw, untoasted cashews (a lot less spendy than pignolis) and nutritional yeast (so it's vegan!). Add a dollop any time you want a hit of herbaceous, garlicky goodness—on sandwiches, in soups and rice and noodle dishes, or with eggs. It's good hot or cold, but adding it to warm foods releases more of that distinctive aroma.

2 cups Thai basil leaves
⅔ cup raw cashews
2 garlic cloves, chopped
1 tablespoon nutritional yeast
1 teaspoon kosher salt
⅓ cup neutral oil, such as
    avocado or canola

In a food processor, combine the basil, cashews, garlic, nutritional yeast, and salt. Pulse a few times to combine, then blend for 15 seconds. Using a spatula, scrape down the sides of the processor and blend for another 5 seconds. With the machine running, slowly add the oil until the pesto turns thick and creamy. Store in an airtight container and use within 5 days.

Basil Basics

I rarely see Thai basil in my regular grocery store, making it one of the very few ingredients I call for in this book that may require a trip to an Asian grocery. If you don't have access to one nearby, try growing your own. Many nurseries now carry Thai basil plants, but you can also root your own from a purchased bunch. Simply pinch off the top three inches of a healthy stem, pull any leaves off the bottom two inches, and pop it into a glass of water. Place it on a sunny windowsill and after about two weeks, you should see a bunch of roots growing from the underwater portion. At that point, it is ready to transfer to a pot or a window box. Let the plant get established before pinching off its top and starting the whole process over again. The donor plant will continue to grow and branch out while its new cuttings grow, ensuring you a ready supply of Thai basil.

Chapter 2

THE BREAKFAST BUFFET

*My Favorite Ways
to Start the Day*

MY MORNING MANTRA IS SIMPLE: FUEL UP, DON'T FILL UP. As tempting as it is to grab a cereal bar or bagel on the way out the door, I find that when I make a good choice for breakfast, it really dictates how I feel and perform for the rest of the day. I've learned the hard way that, for me, a hearty breakfast is pretty much nonnegotiable; it's my best insurance against making questionable choices when the day gets busy, as it inevitably does.

Since I don't get to sit down for a proper lunch as often as I'd like, I often do a breakfast and a half, starting with something substantial first thing, and then doubling down with a protein-rich smoothie or one of the snacks from Chapter 3 (page 72) midmorning to keep me going. Either way, I usually opt for a breakfast that leans more heavily on protein than on carbs, and I try to squeeze in some veggies, too. I find that a serving or two of healthy protein keeps me on an even keel longer—right up through dinner when necessary.

That's why you won't find as many sweet options here as savory, and you'll see eggs in many forms. There is a joke in many Vietnamese households that today's breakfast is just last night's leftovers with an egg on top, but in truth, you could really do a lot worse. Steamed eggs with some of last night's sautéed mushrooms or steamed spinach? A bit of leftover rice stirred together with some kimchi and a fried egg? Or any kind of steamed, roasted, or stir-fried vegetables, rolled up in a carb-free tortilla? Any one of these options will keep you going for hours without spiking your blood sugar. Even when I do make a sweeter breakfast, I make sure there is still plenty of fruit, protein, and fiber on board.

The breakfast options in this chapter range from homey to brunch-worthy, all providing the good fats, protein, and phytonutrients you need to power through a demanding schedule. There are revved-up versions of smoothies, chia pudding, and oatmeal; pancakes and muffins that won't send your blood sugar off the deep end; and so many fun ways to serve eggs, cottage cheese, and yogurt that you'll never get tired of these protein superstars.

THE GLOW-UP GREEN SMOOTHIE

Serves 2

Your skin will thank you when you start the day with a bright-green glassful of antioxidants (the greens) and polyphenols (the grapes), plus a dash of collagen peptides for good measure. For me, the fruit makes this smoothie sweet enough, but you can add a little monk fruit sweetener or liquid stevia if you like. To make this vegan, choose a plant-based collagen powder and swap in coconut yogurt for dairy yogurt. If you're sensitive to caffeine, omit the matcha.

2 cups baby spinach leaves

1 cup frozen mango or
    pineapple chunks

½ cup seedless green grapes

½ cup plain Greek yogurt

½ frozen avocado

2 scoops unflavored collagen
    peptides

1 tablespoon chia seeds

1 teaspoon matcha powder
    (optional)

½ packet (about ½ teaspoon)
    monk fruit sweetener
    (optional)

8 ice cubes

In a blender, combine the spinach, mango, grapes, Greek yogurt, avocado, collagen peptides, chia seeds, matcha powder (if using), monk fruit sweetener (if using), and ice cubes. Add 1 cup of cold water and blend until smooth. Divide between two glasses and enjoy.

✳ *Use chia seeds for my Chia Pudding Cereal (page 53) or the Tapioca Chia Pudding with Mango (page 223).*

Alternative Sweeteners

Most of the recipes in this book are minimally sweetened with unrefined sweeteners like maple syrup, agave nectar, or honey. In some cases, like these smoothies, I add just a pinch of powdered monk fruit (you could also substitute stevia for the monk fruit if that's what you have and like) because it is so powerfully sweet that you don't use enough to add any calories. We just don't know enough about the long-term effects of fake sweeteners that are cooked up in a lab for me to feel completely comfortable with them. On the other hand, just because something is "natural" doesn't mean it's good for you—you could call cocaine or arsenic natural, right? The safest option is to forgo any kind of sweetener when you can, harness the sweetening power of fruit instead, and keep it as unprocessed as possible when a bit of added sweetening is truly called for.

BLUE-*on*-BLUE SMOOTHIE BOWL

Serves 2

I may not be able to pronounce *acai*—yes, yes, I know, it's ah-sah-ee, not ah-see-ai—but I *do* know these superfood berries are one of the healthiest things you can put in a smoothie. It's also a really smart way to make a bowl of yogurt or cottage cheese taste a bit more exciting. Here I've paired frozen acai with blueberries, another superfood, for a deep purple bowl that is ready to be topped with whatever fruit is in season and contrasts nicely with the puree. Add some nuts or seeds and a scant handful (don't go crazy!) of granola for crunch.

2 (3.5-ounce) packets frozen acai puree

1 cup fresh or frozen blueberries

1 cup cottage cheese

½ cup plant-based or dairy milk

FOR SERVING

2 cups sliced fruit

½ cup granola clusters (I like a high-protein blend) or Oat Crumble (page 230) (optional)

2 tablespoons hemp hearts (optional)

Cacao nibs or coconut flakes (optional)

Break the acai into smaller pieces and place in the bowl of a food processor. Add the blueberries, cottage cheese, and ¼ cup of the milk and pulse to combine, then puree until very smooth. If the mixture is too thick, add the remaining milk 1 tablespoon at a time to get the consistency you prefer.

Divide the puree between two shallow bowls. Top with the fruit and your choice of garnishes. Serve immediately.

✳ *Use extra cottage cheese to make a batch of Grab-and-Go Egg Jars (page 59).*

CHIA PUDDING CEREAL

Serves 2

When I saw Kim Kardashian slurping up chia pudding that was a lot soupier than the thick version I usually make, I knew I had to give it a try. Now I've actually come to prefer this version, which is lighter and more refreshing than the usual. The toppings are what make it interesting, so I like to change it up with apple chips, cacao nibs, chopped stone fruit, or any kind of berry. To make a vegan version, use any plant-based milk and a dollop of coconut yogurt.

¼ cup chia seeds

½ teaspoon ground cinnamon

2 cups plant-based or dairy milk

½ cup Greek yogurt or coconut yogurt

1 cup berries of your choice

½ cup sliced almonds

Honey or agave nectar, for drizzling

In a large jar or mixing bowl, combine the chia seeds, cinnamon, and milk. Stir well to combine, then refrigerate for at least 15 minutes or up to overnight. The seeds will soften and swell, but the mixture will remain quite fluid.

To serve, divide the chia mixture between two cereal bowls and top with the yogurt. Sprinkle with the berries and almonds, then drizzle with the honey.

THE MOCHA PROTEIN SMOOTHIE

Serves 1

Premade protein shakes are necessary sometimes, but when I have a few extra minutes in the morning, this much more delicious alternative has a not-too-shabby seventeen grams of protein and no icky added ingredients. For me, a whole banana first thing in the morning is too much sugar, so I have swapped in some frozen avocado instead. It is even creamier than the banana, has lots of good-for-you fats, and complements the flavor of chocolate so well that you won't even notice there is tofu in there!

4 ounces (¼ package) silken tofu
½ cup almond milk
½ frozen avocado
1 scoop chocolate protein powder
1 teaspoon instant espresso powder
1 date
3 ice cubes

In a blender, combine the tofu, almond milk, avocado, protein powder, espresso powder, date, and ice cubes and puree until smooth. Pour into a tall glass and enjoy right away.

CREAMY BANANA OATMEAL *with* PEANUT BUTTER

Serves 2 or 3

Chia seeds and sweet banana give a basic bowl of oatmeal such a creamy texture that makes it so comforting on a cold morning. Oats are surprisingly high in protein, and topped with a big dollop of peanut butter and yogurt, this will send you out the door with about twenty grams of protein that will really stick to your ribs. Dress it up even more with chopped nuts, a little drizzle of maple syrup, and a handful of berries.

1 very ripe banana

1 cup quick-cooking oats

2 tablespoons chia seeds

½ teaspoon ground cinnamon

½ teaspoon kosher salt

2 cups plain, unsweetened almond milk or dairy milk

½ cup fresh or frozen blueberries

2 tablespoons peanut butter per serving

2 tablespoons Greek yogurt per serving

In a large saucepan, use a potato masher or a wooden spoon to mash the banana to a paste. Add the oats, chia seeds, cinnamon, and salt and stir to combine well. Stir in the milk and bring to a simmer over medium heat. Cook, stirring often, until the oatmeal turns thick and creamy, about 3 minutes.

Spoon the oatmeal into bowls, top with blueberries and big dollops of peanut butter and yogurt, and serve right away.

STEAMED EGGS 101

Serves 2

Korean steamed eggs are so fun to make; they come out wobbly, tender, and light as a feather. Once you've mastered the technique, which is really easy, try zhuzhing them up with different flavorings and toppings. I've used everything from leftover miso soup from my takeout sushi order the night before to carrot juice from the juice bar as the liquid. Then I've added sliced mushrooms, tofu, or bits of meat, and every variation comes out great. Steamed eggs are traditionally served over rice, but if you are avoiding carbs in the morning, just skip the rice.

5 large eggs

1 cup chicken or vegetable broth, dashi, or water

½ teaspoon fish sauce or kosher salt

Sesame or canola oil

FOR SERVING

1 cup hot medium- or long-grain rice

2 tablespoons chopped scallion greens

2 tablespoons sesame seeds

Soy sauce, toasted sesame oil, Chili Garlic Oil (page 38), or a combination

Fill a large saucepan or a Dutch oven with about 2 inches of water and bring to a simmer over medium heat.

While the water is heating, break the eggs into a 2-cup glass measuring cup and beat until broken up. Add an equal amount of broth (about 1 cup) and the fish sauce and mix thoroughly but not too vigorously (you don't want to incorporate air in the mixture).

Lightly oil a bowl with a 2-cup capacity, such as a deep cereal bowl, with sesame oil. Pour the egg mixture into the bowl and use a spoon to skim off any bubbles on the surface. Carefully place the bowl in the saucepan, then cover the pan with a tight-fitting lid.

Reduce the heat to medium-low and steam the eggs without lifting the lid for 11 minutes. If they don't appear set in the middle after that time, replace the lid and steam for 1 or 2 more minutes, but don't overcook or they will become rubbery, not soft and delicate.

Divide the rice between two serving bowls and slide the eggs over the top. Sprinkle with scallions and sesame seeds and serve drizzled with your choice of condiments.

Variation: Green Eggs and Ham

Place a big handful (about 1 cup) of baby spinach (or a mix of spinach and baby kale) in a blender. Add a splash of fish sauce or soy sauce, a pinch of mushroom bouillon or salt, and 1 cup of vegetable broth or water. Blend for a full minute until completely combined. Strain into a measuring cup and use a spoon to skim off any bubbles. Proceed as above, using the spinach mixture in place of the broth and stirring in 1 ounce of finely chopped prosciutto or deli ham before steaming.

GRAB-*and*-GO EGG JARS

Serves 4

I'm not really a meal prepper, but I make an exception for these handy egg jars, which are a godsend for mornings when there is absolutely no time to cook. Make a batch at the beginning of the week and you'll have a healthful, savory breakfast ready to pop in the microwave for an instant protein-packed bite all week long. This spinach, Cheddar, and bacon version is a basic template to riff on and it's a great way to use up leftover meat and veggies. I like to include at least one green veggie, a bit of cheese, and something meaty, like mushrooms or cooked sausage—about 1 tablespoon of each per jar—but beyond those basic guidelines, the sky's the limit. Of course, you could bake these in muffin tins, but the little jars are just so much cuter. If you double this recipe, microwave the eggs in two batches, or they won't cook evenly.

¼ cup cooked or thawed frozen spinach, chopped and squeezed dry

¼ cup minced deli ham (about 1 slice)

¼ cup shredded Cheddar cheese

1 cup cottage cheese

4 large eggs

½ teaspoon kosher salt

¼ teaspoon ground black pepper

½ teaspoon garlic powder

Spray four 4-ounce glass jars with nonstick cooking spray (don't skip this step, because the jars are murder to clean otherwise!). Divide the spinach, ham, and Cheddar cheese among the jars.

In a blender, puree the cottage cheese until very smooth, about 15 seconds. Add the eggs, salt, pepper, and garlic powder and pulse once or twice, just until the mixture looks homogeneous with no streaks of yellow.

Pour the egg mixture into the prepared jars, filling them to the rims. Use a skewer or chopstick to poke down to the bottom of the jars, so the eggs cover the mix-ins.

Place the jars on the carousel of your microwave and lay a piece of parchment paper over all four. Microwave on high for 5½ minutes, or until the eggs have set. When everything has cooled, top the jars with lids and refrigerate for up to 5 days. To reheat, remove the lids and microwave for about 40 seconds.

Other Combinations to Try

Sautéed leeks and mushrooms with crumbled goat cheese
Grated zucchini, crumbled feta, and black olives
Chopped broccoli, grated Parmesan, and turkey sausage
Sliced scallions, cream cheese, and minced smoked salmon
Basil, shredded pecorino, and sun-dried tomatoes with a pinch of oregano

HUEVOS RANCHEROS BREAKFAST BURRITOS

Makes 2 wraps, serving 2 or 4, depending on appetite

Start your day with one of these low-carb zucchini "tortillas" filled with black beans, steak, avocado, and salsa, and you will be well on your way toward your five daily servings of veggies. A little bit of cornmeal in the wrapper enhances the tortilla illusion without loading you up on carbs. For a dinner alternative, double the recipe, nestle the wraps in a baking dish, swap the steak for shredded chicken, and cover with enchilada sauce. Sprinkle with more cheese and bake until bubbly!

ZUCCHINI "TORTILLAS"

1 medium zucchini (about 9 ounces), shredded

3 eggs, lightly beaten

½ cup fine- or medium-grind cornmeal

1 teaspoon kosher salt

½ teaspoon ground black pepper

½ teaspoon garlic powder

½ cup shredded Cheddar or Mexican cheese blend

FOR SERVING

1 cup cooked black beans, drained

¼ cup plain Greek or regular yogurt

Juice of 1 small lime

4 to 6 ounces leftover steak or deli roast beef, sliced

1 ripe avocado, sliced

½ cup prepared salsa

Hot sauce (optional)

Preheat the oven to 400°F. Line a rimmed baking sheet with parchment paper. Lightly spray the parchment paper with nonstick cooking spray.

Spread the grated zucchini on a kitchen towel, roll it up tightly, and then wring the towel over the sink, squeezing out as much moisture as possible. Transfer the zucchini to a mixing bowl and add the eggs, cornmeal, salt, pepper, and garlic powder. Mix until well combined, then stir in the cheese.

Spoon the zucchini mixture onto the prepared baking sheet, making a mound at each end. Starting from the center of each mound, use the back of the spoon to evenly spread the mixture into a circle, making the tortillas as thin as possible.

Bake the tortillas until their tops look mostly dry, about 5 minutes. Carefully lift the parchment paper and tortillas from the baking sheet and place them on the counter. Lightly spray the baking sheet with nonstick spray. Flip the parchment paper and tortillas onto the baking sheet, tortilla-side down, and peel off the parchment paper. Return the tortillas to the oven until they turn golden brown, about 5 minutes.

While the tortillas bake, place the beans in a small microwave-safe bowl and microwave on high for 1 minute to heat through. In another small bowl, stir the yogurt and lime juice together until smooth and well combined.

Spoon the beans onto the tortillas and top with the steak and avocado slices. Add a few spoonfuls of salsa, drizzle with the yogurt, and add a splash of hot sauce, if using. Roll up the tortillas, slice them in half on the diagonal, and serve hot.

✳ *Use up the can of black beans in the big steak salad on page 145.*

KIMCHI FRIED RICE

Serves 4

Here's a classic example of the Vietnamese adage "Today's breakfast is last night's leftovers . . . with an egg on it!" This is just about the simplest fried rice recipe there is, because the kimchi itself is so flavorful you don't need to add a lot of seasonings. When the creamy egg yolk mixes with the savory kimchi, it's just an extremely comforting thing to eat. It's also a great use for older kimchi that may be hanging around in your fridge because you want plenty of sour tang. Don't throw out the kimchi liquid, it is what gives the rice so much flavor.

8 scallions

4 tablespoons neutral oil, such as avocado or canola

¼ teaspoon kosher salt

1 cup drained kimchi, liquid reserved, cut in small pieces

3 cups cooked jasmine rice, preferably a day old

4 eggs

2 teaspoons sesame oil

¼ cup furikake, homemade (page 32) or store-bought

Chili Garlic Oil (page 38), for drizzling, (optional)

Separate the white and green parts of the scallions. Slice the white parts about ¼ inch thick. Thinly slice the green parts of 2 scallions on the bias (reserve the rest for another use) and set aside.

Heat 2 tablespoons of the oil in a large wok or skillet over medium-high heat. Add the white parts of the scallions, sprinkle with the salt, and quickly stir-fry until softened and starting to brown, about 2 minutes. Add the kimchi and a few tablespoons of its liquid and cook together for a minute. Add the rice, toss to combine, and stir-fry until heated through, about 5 minutes. Reduce the heat to medium-low and let the rice cook without stirring to brown the bottom while you fry the eggs.

Heat the remaining 2 tablespoons of oil in a large, nonstick skillet over medium-high heat. Break the eggs into the skillet and fry until the edges are getting brown and crisp, 2 or 3 minutes. Reduce the heat to medium, cover the pan, and cook until the yolks are set to your liking, about 2 minutes.

Drizzle the sesame oil over the fried rice and toss to distribute the browned rice. Scoop the fried rice into 4 serving bowls and slide a fried egg onto each serving. Sprinkle with some of the scallion greens and the furikake. Drizzle with a bit of the chili garlic oil if desired. Serve hot.

KIMCHI FRIED RICE

page 61

APPLE WALNUT MUFFINS

Makes 12 large muffins

Not too sweet with a surprisingly light texture, these gluten-free muffins are literally packed with fruit, making them a good after-school snack or lunchbox addition if your school allows nuts. The flavor of the muffins improves if you refrigerate the batter overnight, so you can mix them up one day and scoop and bake them the next morning. The house will smell great and you will look like a superstar! I leave the apples unpeeled, but if you don't like their chewy texture, go ahead and peel them.

2 cups almond flour

1 cup rice flour

1 teaspoon baking soda

1½ teaspoons ground cinnamon

1 teaspoon kosher salt

2 eggs

1 cup applesauce

½ cup plain Greek yogurt

½ cup maple syrup

2 Granny Smith apples, cored and cut into small dice

1½ cups toasted walnuts, chopped

2 tablespoons coarse sugar, such as Sugar in the Raw

Preheat the oven to 350°F. Line a 12-cup muffin tin with paper liners.

In a medium bowl, whisk together the almond flour, rice flour, baking soda, cinnamon, and salt. In a large mixing bowl, whisk together the eggs, applesauce, yogurt, and maple syrup until well combined.

Add the flour mixture to the applesauce mixture and stir with a rubber spatula until well incorporated. Stir in the diced apple and 1 cup of the walnuts.

Spoon the batter into the prepared muffin tin, filling each cup right to the top of the liner. Sprinkle the remaining ½ cup of walnuts over the tops of the muffins and dust each one with a pinch of sugar.

Bake the muffins on the center rack of the oven until the tops spring back when pressed and a toothpick inserted in the center of one of the muffins comes out clean, about 30 minutes. Tip the muffins out onto a wire rack and let cool completely before serving.

THANKSGIVING BAKED OAT MUFFINS

Makes 6 muffins

Here's another gluten-free option that straddles the line between a conventional muffin and baked oatmeal. You'll get notes of candied yams, pecan pie, and cranberry sauce in every bite—enjoy one or two with some turkey bacon, and all you'll be missing are the mashed potatoes and gravy!

¾ cup pecans

1 medium sweet potato (about 6 ounces)

½ cup almond or regular milk

1 large egg

1½ cups oat flour (see My Tip)

¼ cup packed brown sugar

½ teaspoon kosher salt

½ teaspoon ground allspice

1 teaspoon baking powder

½ cup dried cranberries

Preheat the oven to 350°F. Line every other cup of a 12-cup muffin tin with paper liners.

While the oven preheats, spread the pecans in a single layer on a baking sheet and toast them until they turn lightly golden, about 8 minutes. Transfer to a plate and, when they have cooled, coarsely chop them. Set aside.

Poke the sweet potato in several places with the tip of a knife to release steam and microwave on high until it is very soft, about 6 minutes.

When the sweet potato is cool enough to handle, scoop the flesh into a large mixing bowl and mash well with a fork. Add the milk and egg and stir together with the fork.

In a separate large bowl, whisk together the oat flour, brown sugar, salt, allspice, and baking powder. Add the flour mixture to the sweet potato mixture and stir with a rubber spatula until well incorporated. Stir in the cranberries and ½ cup of the chopped pecans.

Spoon the batter into the prepared muffin tin, filling each cup right to the top of the liner. Sprinkle the remaining ¼ cup of pecans over the tops of the muffins.

Bake the muffins on the center rack of the oven until the tops spring back when pressed and a toothpick inserted in the center of one of the muffins comes out clean, about 25 minutes. Tip the muffins out onto a wire rack and serve warm or at room temperature.

My Tip: No need to buy oat flour. Just whiz regular old-fashioned rolled oats in your blender until reduced to a fairly fine powder.

✳ *Save any extra oat flour for rolling out Chewy Chocolate Nut Bars (page 88); toss the dried cranberries in the Five-Spice Snack Mix (page 84) or the Bark Bites with Quinoa Crunchies (page 240).*

HEART-Y STRAWBERRY PANCAKES

Serves 4

Pancake cereal—tiny dots of pancake batter cooked on a griddle and served in a bowl with milk—was one of my most viral videos and they were a lot of fun to eat, if not exactly the breakfast of champions. These silver-dollar-sized pancakes are just as fun to eat and, better yet, they are gluten-free and full of protein. The strawberries make them so sweet that they need only a kiss of syrup to deliver that total pancake experience. Just make sure to cook the pancakes over low heat to prevent the berries from scorching. If you have a plastic squeeze bottle, it makes portioning out the batter really easy.

1 pint strawberries, the smallest you can find (see My Tip)

1 cup rolled oats (preferably gluten-free)

1 cup cottage cheese

2 eggs

¼ cup plant-based or dairy milk

¼ cup plus 2 tablespoons maple syrup

½ teaspoon baking powder

½ teaspoon ground cinnamon or grated lemon zest

Neutral oil, such as avocado or canola

Hull the strawberries and cut each one lengthwise into four slices. (If your berries are large, you may get five or six slices from each.) Place the strawberries in a small bowl.

Place the oats in a blender and whiz until they're reduced to a powdery, flour-like consistency, about 30 seconds. Pour the oats into a small bowl (no need to clean out the blender) and add the cottage cheese to the blender. Whiz until smooth, 15 to 20 seconds, then add the eggs, milk, ¼ cup of the maple syrup, baking powder, cinnamon, and the pulverized oats. Blend until well combined.

Lightly oil a griddle or a large nonstick skillet and place over medium heat. When the griddle is hot enough to evaporate a bead of water dropped on the surface, reduce the heat to medium-low. One at a time, place a strawberry slice on the griddle and immediately spoon on just enough batter to cover the berry, about 2 teaspoons. Repeat until the surface of the griddle is covered.

Cook until the pancakes have set enough to flip, about 2 minutes, then use a thin spatula (an offset spatula works well) to turn them berry-side up. Continue cooking until they turn golden brown on the second side, 2 to 3 minutes (there shouldn't be any steam emerging from the sides of the pancakes). Transfer the pancakes to a plate and keep warm. Continue making pancakes until the batter is used up.

While the last batch of pancakes is cooking, combine the remaining sliced strawberries in a small bowl with the remaining 2 tablespoons of maple syrup. Divide the pancakes among serving plates and pass the syrupy berries at the table for topping.

My Tip: If you can't find small strawberries (farmers' markets will be your best bet), just use bigger berries and a tablespoon more batter for each pancake.

✻ *Use your extra strawberries in the Vietnamese Fruit Cocktail dessert (page 224) or on a Blue-on-Blue Smoothie Bowl (page 50).*

FULLY LOADED BAGEL SPREAD

Makes 1½ cups

There is something so indulgent about a bagel piled high with cream cheese, salmon, and all the fixings, but it also makes me want to crawl back into bed for the rest of the day! A schmear of this make-ahead spread on half a bagel or bagel chips gives me all the brunchy feels without all the fat and carbs. Mixing just a little bit of cream cheese with higher-protein, lower-fat cottage cheese makes it plenty rich and creamy. Spread on a slice of cucumber instead of the bagel, it also makes a nice canapé.

4 ounces smoked salmon

2 tablespoons finely chopped red onion

1 tablespoon capers, rinsed, drained, and finely chopped (optional but nice) plus more for serving

1 tablespoon chopped fresh dill

Zest and juice from ½ small lemon (about 2 teaspoons juice)

2 ounces (one-quarter of an 8-ounce brick) reduced-fat cream cheese

½ cup cottage cheese

½ teaspoon kosher salt

Toasted bagel halves or bagel chips

Tomato slices, for serving

Flaky salt, for serving

With a large, sharp knife, finely mince the smoked salmon. Transfer to a mixing bowl and add the onion, capers (if using), dill, and lemon zest and juice. Toss with a fork to combine thoroughly.

Combine the cream cheese and cottage cheese in the bowl of a food processor or a blender. Blend until very smooth, scraping down the sides once or twice. Add the mixture to the bowl with the salmon and mix gently with a rubber spatula until well combined. Taste for seasoning and add salt as desired; depending on how salty your salmon is, you may not need any at all.

Spread on a toasted bagel half or a bagel chip and top with a tomato slice and a few capers and a pinch of flaky salt.

❀ *Finish off the cream cheese by making Spinach Artichoke Dip (page 89) or a Gotcha-Gordon Bell Pepper "Sandwich" (page 105).*

BREAKFAST FLATBREADS

Serves 4

Pizza for breakfast? Yes, please! You'll want to bookmark this super-simple flatbread because its protein-rich dough is equally good cut into squares for cocktail nibbles or even thrown on the grill for all kinds of fun summer pizza improvs. Topped with just a bit of cream cheese for richness and a sprinkle of Parm because YUM, this is an alternative to bacon, eggs, and toast that feels a lot more special.

FLATBREADS

1½ cups all-purpose flour

1 cup plain Greek yogurt

½ teaspoon kosher salt

½ teaspoon baking powder

2 tablespoons coarse-grind cornmeal

4 ounces regular or reduced-fat cream cheese

4 strips turkey bacon or prosciutto, cut crosswise into thin pieces

4 to 8 large eggs

Kosher salt and ground black pepper

4 tablespoons grated Parmesan cheese

Chopped chives or Chili Garlic Oil (page 38), for serving

Preheat the oven to 450°F.

In a large mixing bowl, stir together the flour, yogurt, salt, and baking powder to make a soft dough. Turn the dough onto a lightly floured surface and knead a few times until the dough is smooth. Cover it with a kitchen towel and let it rest for about 15 minutes.

Sprinkle two large baking sheets with the cornmeal. Divide the dough into four portions. With a rolling pin, roll out the dough to create four oval flatbreads, each measuring about 4 × 8 inches. Carefully place the flatbreads on the prepared baking sheets.

Place the cream cheese in a small microwave-safe bowl and microwave on high in 30-second increments, stirring after each interval, until it becomes fluid enough to spread, about 90 seconds total. Divide the cream cheese among the flatbreads and spread it to within ½ inch of the edges. Top with the bacon pieces and bake for 5 minutes.

Remove the flatbreads from the oven and carefully break an egg or two onto the center of each one. Sprinkle with salt, pepper, and Parmesan. Return the flatbreads to the oven and bake until they're puffed and golden and the eggs are set, another 6 or 7 minutes.

Serve sprinkled with the chopped chives or a drizzle of chili garlic oil.

✺ *If you didn't finish off the bunch of chives, this is a perfect opportunity to whip up some Green Goddess Dressing (page 139).*

Chapter 3

SNACKY THINGS

Energy-Boosting Snacks, Spreads, and Sammies

WE ALL HAVE MOMENTS WHEN WE NEED A LITTLE SOMETHING to tide us over, give us a bit of energy, and not blow the bank on carbs and sugar, whether it's the midmorning munchies, the "Oops, I forgot to eat lunch" hangries, or the predinner need to nibble. For times like those, this chapter's got you covered.

If you are like me, there are plenty of days when you hit the ground running and don't stop going until the sun has begun to set. Way too often, this means working right through lunchtime. It also means that by the time dinner rolls around, I am beyond ravenous. Having some turbocharged snack foods, a tote-along sandwich, or something to tide me over while I make a meal for my family is essential, and a great strategy for staying on the straight and narrow all day long.

The recipes that follow all provide a hit of healthy nutrients and protein just when you need them most, and they do double duty as good-for-them after-school snacks for your kids. All but a few can be made ahead of time so you can recharge with something nutrient-dense and delicious in as little time as it takes to rip open a bag of chips. Plus, you'll feel a lot better after eating some veggies with Broccoli Hummus (page 90) or hydrating with a Green Goddess Juice (page 78) than you would after gobbling down a granola bar (or an order of fries).

Try serving my lightened-up Spinach Artichoke Dip (page 89) on game day or my Five-Spice Snack Mix (page 84) with predinner cocktails. Tuck a freshly baked fruit-and-nut oat bar (page 87) in your backpack. Treat yourself to a midafternoon Golden Turmeric Latte (page 81). Any one of these will give you the boost you need without a sugary crash.

DRAGON FRUIT SMOOTHIE

Serves 1

Creamy and refreshing, this thirst-quenching smoothie tastes like the most exotic creamsicle you've ever had. I make it with coconut milk to keep the tropical theme going, but any nondairy or dairy milk would be just fine here. If you can't find purple dragon fruit, don't stress; it won't be as vividly colored but it will still taste great.

1 small or ½ large fresh purple dragon fruit (about 8 ounces), peeled, or frozen chunks

¼ cup coconut milk

2 tablespoons fresh orange juice

6 fresh mint leaves, plus a sprig for garnish

4 ice cubes

Cut the dragon fruit into chunks and place in a blender. Add the coconut milk, orange juice, mint leaves, and ice cubes and blend until smooth. Garnish with the mint sprig and serve immediately.

GREEN GODDESS JUICE

Serves 4

So many of the green juices we get outside the home contain tons of hidden sugar in the form of pear nectar or apple juice concentrate. I find that just a little bit of apple—about a quarter of a Granny Smith per serving—is plenty of sweetness for this refreshing blend, which is super hydrating thanks to the coconut water. It won't be as clear as a drink made in the juicer, and that's okay; you're getting all that good fiber (and spending much less time cleaning your juicer!) instead. This tastes best cold and is great after a workout.

1 green apple, such as Granny Smith, peeled and cut into chunks

3 unpeeled Persian cucumbers, or 1 small hothouse cucumber, peeled and seeded

2 packed cups (about 2½ ounces) baby kale or spinach

2 cups coconut water

20 fresh mint leaves

1-inch piece of fresh ginger, peeled and chopped

¼ teaspoon kosher salt

Combine all the ingredients in a blender and blend until completely smooth. Drink right away or refrigerate until ready to serve. Shake well before pouring into glasses.

GOLDEN TURMERIC LATTE

Serves 2

Most packaged chai or golden latte mixes are way too sweet for my palate. This one gets a bit of bite from the ginger and cayenne pepper, and it tastes smooth, creamy, and just sweet enough. It's a luxurious way to get your daily dose of antioxidants!

2 cups plant-based or dairy milk

2 teaspoons Solid-Gold Turmeric Paste (page 29)

2 teaspoons agave nectar, or to taste

1 (2-inch) cinnamon stick or ¼ teaspoon ground cinnamon

¼ teaspoon ground cardamom

Teeny pinch cayenne pepper (optional)

In a deep saucepan over medium heat, bring the milk to a gentle simmer. Add the remaining ingredients and reduce the heat to low. Simmer until it smells yummy, about 3 minutes. Whip the mixture with a milk frother if you have one (or a hand whisk if not) until it is foamy. Using a fine-mesh strainer, strain into two mugs and enjoy warm.

✴ *Blend 1 to 3 teaspoons of Solid-Gold Turmeric Paste (page 29) with 1 cup of well-chilled coconut water for 15 seconds, then strain into a glass with ice for a super-hydrating drink that is perfect after a long hike on a hot day. Or make the Wellness Soup on page 123.*

ULTRA-UMAMI KALE CHIPS

Makes about 2 cups

Crispy kale chips aren't new, but when you are craving something that's salty, crunchy, and actually good for you, they're the best. I'm always amazed when I see how pricey store-bought kale chips are, because they are just about the easiest thing ever to prepare in the air fryer and cost just pennies to make. These are seasoned simply with mushroom bouillon powder, but they don't really taste mushroomy per se—just incredibly savory and a little salty. Crumble a handful onto a rice bowl or even soup for a little extra texture and zing.

½ bunch curly kale (about 8 big leaves), stems removed, leaves torn into large pieces

Olive or avocado oil cooking spray

1 teaspoon mushroom bouillon powder

1 tablespoon grated pecorino cheese

Place the kale in a large bowl and spray lightly with the olive oil cooking spray. Toss well, spray again, and toss one more time. You want a light coating of oil on every piece of kale, so give the leaves another spritz if needed. Sprinkle the leaves with the mushroom bouillon powder and pecorino, and use your hands to turn and toss the leaves to coat them evenly with the seasonings.

Air-fry the kale at 325°F for 8 minutes, tossing the leaves halfway through. Let them cool at room temperature (they will crisp up as they stand), then store in an airtight container for up to a couple of weeks.

❋ *Use mushroom bouillon powder to up your steak frites game (page 180).*

FIVE-SPICE SNACK MIX

Makes about 4 cups

When you start with a tin of roasted mixed nuts, it takes just minutes in the oven or an air fryer to get them extra crisp, toasty, and just a teeny bit sweet. Add any dried fruit you like and a small handful of mini crackers or even Chex cereal for an anytime snack or a party nibble.

1 (10-ounce) can mixed nuts or about 2 cups peanuts (not dry roasted)

1 tablespoon neutral oil, such as avocado or canola

4 teaspoons sugar

2 teaspoons kosher salt

1 teaspoon Chinese five-spice powder, pumpkin pie spice, or ground allspice

¼ teaspoon cayenne pepper, or to taste

2 cups Crushed Chickpea Crunchers (facing page)

1 cup dried cranberries or golden raisins

½ cup sesame sticks or other small, crunchy tidbits

Preheat the oven to 350°F.

Place the nuts in a large bowl, drizzle with the oil, and toss well to coat. Add the sugar, salt, five-spice powder, and cayenne and toss again. Spread the nuts in a single layer on a rimmed baking sheet and bake until the nuts smell toasty, about 15 minutes, stirring them once about halfway through.

Scrape the nuts into a bowl and stir in the chickpeas, dried cranberries, and sesame sticks. Let cool. The mix can be stored in an airtight container for up to several weeks.

CRUSHED CHICKPEA CRUNCHERS

Makes about 2 cups

If you like roasted chickpeas, but don't have the patience to babysit them for 40 minutes in the oven, you're going to love this hack. I discovered that pressing down on the chickpeas to flatten them a bit not only cuts the cooking time significantly but also yields many more crunchy, crispy bits, too. This recipe offers a pretty basic flavor profile, but once you've got the method down, go ahead and season yours with anything from herbes de Provence to taco mix to some delish homemade furikake (page 32). Then eat them out of hand, toss a handful onto a salad, or use them to garnish a bowl of hummus for a little extra protein and texture.

1 (15-ounce) can chickpeas, rinsed, drained, and patted dry
1½ teaspoons garlic powder
1½ teaspoons kosher salt
1 teaspoon smoked paprika
1 teaspoon ground cumin

Preheat your air fryer to 380°F.

Spread the chickpeas on the rack or in the basket of your air fryer. Using the bottom of a glass or the heel of your hand, press down gently on the chickpeas to flatten them a bit; you don't want to completely pulverize them, just pop the skins and spread them out slightly. It's okay if they are not all exactly the same thickness.

Air-fry the chickpeas for 8 minutes, tossing them once about halfway through. Sprinkle with the seasonings and let cool before transferring to an airtight container. They will keep for weeks but they lose their crunch after a few days.

❄ *Make a double batch and use the extra chickpeas to top a salad, or in the Five-Spice Snack Mix (facing page) or the Seven-Layer Mediterranean Dip (page 93).*

CHEWY
CHOCOLATE
NUT BARS

page 88

NSFW OAT BARS

Makes 8 bars or 16 squares

NSFW stands for nuts, seeds, fruit, and wheat germ (why, what were you thinking?), and together they make a filling, wholesome, portable snack bar with a lot less sugar than store-bought granola bars. They're also a great way to use up baking odds and ends. Just make sure the total amount of fruit, nuts, and seeds equals about 2 cups. As these bake, your whole house will smell like oatmeal cookies!

1 cup plain low-fat yogurt

2 tablespoons honey

1 cup quick-cooking oats

¼ cup wheat germ

1 cup dried fruit (chopped apricots, figs, dried cranberries, etc.)

1 cup chopped nuts and seeds (pepitas, sunflower seeds, walnuts, pecans, etc.)

1 teaspoon ground cinnamon

½ teaspoon baking soda

½ teaspoon kosher salt

Preheat the oven to 350°F. Spray a 9 × 9-inch pan with nonstick cooking spray or line with parchment paper.

In a medium bowl, combine the yogurt, honey, oats, and wheat germ and mix with a rubber spatula until well combined. Add the fruit, nuts, seeds, cinnamon, baking soda, and salt. Mix thoroughly to make a fairly stiff dough.

Using the spatula, spread and press the mixture in an even layer in the prepared pan. Bake until the oat mixture is set and turns light brown around the edges, about 35 minutes. Let the mixture cool completely in the pan before cutting into bars or squares.

❋ *Didn't get around to eating them all? Crumble leftover bars and toast them in the air fryer until crisp, then use them to top yogurt, chia pudding, or a fruit salad. Or dip a banana half in chocolate ganache (page 227), roll it in the crispy oat bits, and freeze for a healthier take on drumsticks!*

CHEWY CHOCOLATE NUT BARS

Makes 9 3-inch bars

One of the least-used features of an air fryer is the dehydrate function, and if you haven't gone down that road yet, here is a great reason to give it a go. Dehydrating turns these slightly soft, sticky bars into chewy, chocolatey treats with the consistency of a Tootsie Roll—if those came stuffed with nuts and chia seeds instead of corn syrup and artificial sweeteners. The chocolate chips are optional here, but it's just a handful and they contribute a fun burst of indulgent flavor.

20 large dates (preferably Medjool), pitted

¾ teaspoon kosher salt

4 tablespoons peanut butter powder, plus more for dusting

2 tablespoons cocoa powder

1 cup raw, untoasted cashews or almonds, or a combination

¼ cup mini chocolate chips (optional)

2 tablespoons chia seeds

½ cup oat flour (see My Tip, page 65)

Place the dates in the bowl of a food processor. With the motor running, add about 1½ tablespoons of water and the salt, and continue to process until the dates are reduced to a thick, stiff paste. Add more water by the half teaspoon if needed to help blend the dates to a paste.

Scrape the date paste into a mixing bowl and add 3 tablespoons of the peanut butter powder and the cocoa. Use a stiff spatula to work the dry ingredients into the paste, switching to your hands as needed to knead the mixture until fully incorporated and smooth.

Dust a work surface with the remaining 1 tablespoon of peanut butter powder. Turn the date mixture onto the work surface and use a rolling pin to flatten it into a disc. Sprinkle the nuts, chocolate chips (if using), and chia seeds over the surface and knead a few times to distribute the ingredients throughout the dough. Sprinkle the work surface with more peanut butter powder if it gets too sticky.

Dust both sides of the dough generously with the oat flour and place on a piece of parchment paper. Use a rolling pin to flatten the dough into a 6 × 9-inch rectangle, and square off the edges as well as you can. Cut the sheet into thirds lengthwise, then into thirds crosswise to make nine rectangular bars.

Transfer the bars to your air fryer and dehydrate for 12 hours. Store the finished bars at room temperature for up to 2 weeks.

SPINACH ARTICHOKE DIP

Makes about 3 cups

If you are like me, this warm, cheesy, indulgent dip is a must-order whenever it appears on a restaurant menu, but when it's dripping with cheese and mayo, it definitely falls under the "guilty pleasure" heading. Because it's such a crowd-pleaser, though, I thought it was worth trying to rehabilitate it, and I'm so glad I did! My version is just as creamy and rich as the original, but without a drop of mayonnaise in sight. The artichokes I use are preserved in brine, which adds some salt; if you use water-packed ones, you might need to season the dip a bit more generously.

1 cup cottage cheese

2 ounces reduced-fat cream cheese

½ cup grated Parmesan cheese

2 tablespoons brine from the artichoke jar or vegetable broth

½ teaspoon garlic powder

½ teaspoon kosher salt

1 (10-ounce) package frozen chopped spinach, thawed and squeezed dry

1 (12-ounce) jar artichokes (about 1¼ cups), drained and roughly chopped

Raw veggies or pita chips, for serving

Preheat the oven to 375°F.

Place the cottage cheese, cream cheese, Parmesan, and artichoke brine in the bowl of a food processor. Blend for 1 minute until smooth, scraping down the sides of the processor once or twice. If the mixture is too thick (it should be fluid but not runny), blend in a bit more brine.

Add the garlic powder, salt, and spinach and pulse on and off until well combined. Scrape down the sides of the processor again, add the artichokes, and pulse five times to combine.

Transfer the mixture to a shallow 1-quart baking dish. Bake on the top shelf until lightly browned and bubbly, about 15 minutes. Serve warm with chips or veggies.

❄ *Any unused cream cheese can be used in the Fully Loaded Bagel Spread (page 69) or on Breakfast Flatbreads (page 70).*

BROCCOLI HUMMUS

Makes about 2 cups

For most people, chickpeas are the defining ingredient of hummus, but for me, it's the tahini. For this veggie-forward dip, I prefer creamy butter beans because their mild personality lets the other flavors shine through. This hummus gets its subtle, nutty undertones from shallot oil, an ingredient you will have at the ready if you've been stocking your pantry with fried shallots, although extra-virgin olive oil is also delicious here. If you have cooked broccoli in your fridge (as I nearly always do), you can pull this together in about two minutes flat.

1 small fresh broccoli crown, cut into small florets, or 2 cups cooked broccoli

1 cup canned butter beans, drained

2 tablespoons tahini

2 tablespoons fresh lemon juice

1 large garlic clove, chopped

1 teaspoon kosher salt

¼ cup shallot-infused oil (page 33) or extra-virgin olive oil, plus more for drizzling

2 tablespoons Fried Shallots (page 33)

1 pinch hot pepper flakes (optional)

If you're using fresh broccoli, bring a large saucepan of salted water to a boil over medium-high heat. Add the broccoli and cook until it is quite tender when pierced with a fork, about 5 minutes. Drain well.

Place the cooked broccoli in the bowl of a food processor. Add the butter beans, tahini, lemon juice, garlic, and salt. Blend until pureed and fairly smooth. With the motor running, add the shallot oil and blend until smooth and creamy.

Serve topped with a drizzle of oil, the fried shallots, and a pinch of hot pepper flakes, if desired.

Use the rest of the canned butter beans in Mahi Mahi Tostadas with Fruity Slaw (page 163), in place of the canned Great Northern beans.

SEVEN-LAYER MEDITERRANEAN DIP

Makes about 6 cups

If a Tex-Mex seven-layer dip is your go-to party dish, you'll want to add this brighter, lighter version to your repertoire ASAP. It makes an ideal game-day snack served with chips or veggies, or serve it with mini pitas so everyone can scoop up their own baby sandwiches. A layer of air-fried crispy chickpeas adds a nice texture reminiscent of a fattoush salad, but if you don't want to add that extra step, regular chickpeas work just fine.

MEDITERRANEAN "SALSA"

2 plum tomatoes, seeded and cut into small dice

2 Persian cucumbers or ½ hothouse cucumber, seeded and cut into small dice

½ small red onion, cut into small dice

1 teaspoon za'atar or dried oregano

1 teaspoon kosher salt

Juice of 1 lemon

1 cup plain Greek yogurt

1 garlic clove

½ teaspoon kosher salt

1 (8-ounce) container hummus, any flavor

2 ripe avocados, mashed (or 1 cup prepared guacamole)

1 cup crumbled feta cheese

1 cup Crushed Chickpea Crunchers (page 85) or canned chickpeas, drained

½ cup pitted green or black olives, slivered

Pita chips or crudités, for serving

In a small bowl, combine the salsa ingredients and set aside. In a separate small bowl, stir the yogurt until smooth. Grate the garlic clove directly into the yogurt, add the salt, and stir to combine.

To assemble the dip, spread the hummus evenly over the bottom of a 1-quart dish or glass bowl. Next, spread a layer of mashed avocado evenly over the hummus and top with the garlicky yogurt. Spoon the salsa over the yogurt, making sure to include some of its lemony juices (this will help season the lower layers of the dip). Top with the crumbled feta, chickpeas, and slivered olives. Serve with the pita chips or crudités. Store the well-covered leftovers in the refrigerator for up to 3 days.

✺   *The next day, after all the flavors have mingled, this dip is delicious spooned onto a piece of toasted sourdough for breakfast or a midafternoon snack.*

"FREE" PORK *and* MANGO SPRING ROLLS, DAD'S WAY

Makes 8 spring rolls

When we owned our family restaurant, my father loved to slip a free order of spring rolls to his favorite customers—and now I am gifting them to you! Dad's version is the trusty classic, made with pork, vermicelli noodles, and mango; I keep the carbs in check by swapping in bean sprouts for most of the vermicelli noodles and using shrimp in place of the pork in the variation that follows. You could also substitute grilled chicken thighs or even tofu for the protein; the mango and dipping sauce make just about anything they are served with taste amazing!

8 rice-paper rounds

8 red or green butter lettuce leaves or a handful of spring mix

2 ounces vermicelli noodles, cooked and drained

2 Persian cucumbers or ½ hothouse cucumber, cut into 2-inch-long strips

Leaves from ½ bunch mint

2 red Thai chiles, thinly sliced (optional)

8 ounces Vietnamese Pork Tenderloin (page 177) or other cooked pork or protein

2 ripe mangos, peeled and cut into thin strips

PEANUT DIPPING SAUCE

2 tablespoons peanut butter

2 tablespoons hoisin sauce

⅓ cup plant-based or dairy milk

Place the rice-paper rounds and a large, shallow bowl of water next to your work surface. Working with one rice paper at a time, slide each paper quickly into the water, then immediately rotate it through the water to wet the entire surface just until pliable. Shake off the excess water and lay the rice paper on your work surface. Place a few pieces of lettuce at the far edge of the rice paper and top with some of the noodles, 2 cucumber strips, 4 or 5 mint leaves, a bit of chile (if using), and 2 strips of pork.

Working quickly but carefully, fold the sides of the rice paper in over the fillings, then roll the paper toward you to enclose the filling. Tuck 3 strips of mango under the rolled portion, then continue rolling the rice paper toward you to make a neat, tight roll. Repeat with the remaining rice papers and filling to make 8 spring rolls.

To make the dipping sauce: In a small bowl, stir the peanut butter, hoisin sauce, and milk until smooth and thoroughly combined.

Serve the spring rolls at room temperature with the peanut dipping sauce on the side.

✳ *Finish off the package of rice-paper rounds by making Firecracker Salmon (page 100).*

Variation: Skinny Spring Rolls, My Way

For the pork, substitute 16 large shrimp, cooked and halved, and use 2 cups of fresh bean sprouts in place of the vermicelli noodles. Assemble as above, using 4 shrimp halves for each spring roll. For each spring roll, add the shrimp last so they are visible through the wrapper.

TOFU DUMPLINGS *in* CHILI GARLIC OIL

Makes 2 dozen dumplings

I won't pretend that this is the most spontaneous of snacks, but the recipe makes a generous quantity with more than enough to freeze. Once the dumplings are filled and frozen, you can pull out as few or as many at a time as you want, whenever you want. You can, of course, serve them in broth with noodles and vegetables to make them more of a meal or with The Very Best Dumpling Sauce (page 41) for dipping, but I really like them on their own, just drizzled with a bit of chili garlic oil and sprinkled with scallions. Four or five of these slippery devils make a really good snack, or the first course of a multiple-dish spread.

½ cup chopped napa cabbage

1 teaspoon kosher salt

1 (14-ounce) package firm tofu

½ cup chopped fresh shiitake mushrooms

6 or 8 scallions (white and green parts), sliced

1 tablespoon cornstarch

1 tablespoon soy sauce

1 tablespoon toasted sesame oil

1 teaspoon rice vinegar

½ teaspoon grated fresh ginger

½ teaspoon grated garlic

½ teaspoon sugar

¼ teaspoon ground black pepper

1 package square wonton wrappers

FOR SERVING

Chili Garlic Oil (page 38)

Sesame seeds

Chopped scallion greens

Place the chopped cabbage in a colander and toss with the salt. Set the colander in the sink for about 15 minutes to allow the cabbage to release some of its liquid.

Slice the tofu into four slabs and place them on a kitchen towel. Top with another towel and place a weight, such as a heavy skillet, on top for a few minutes to press out some of the moisture.

Crumble the tofu into a mixing bowl and add the drained cabbage, shiitakes, scallions, cornstarch, soy sauce, sesame oil, rice vinegar, ginger, garlic, sugar, and pepper. With clean hands, mix thoroughly to distribute the seasonings and cornstarch throughout the filling.

Line a rimmed baking sheet with parchment paper. To form the dumplings, place about 1 teaspoon of filling in the center of a wrapper. With your fingers, wet the edges with water and fold the wrapper in half diagonally to form a triangle. Press out any air around the filling, then squeeze the edges firmly together to seal. Now hold the dumpling in both hands with the fold on top and bring the two corners together in a circle, pressing them together to seal. Repeat (and repeat and repeat!) with the remaining filling. Arrange the dumplings on the prepared baking sheet as you go.

Place the formed dumplings in the freezer until they are firm, about 2 hours, then transfer them to heavy-duty freezer bags. The frozen dumplings will keep for up to 3 months.

To serve, drop the frozen dumplings into salted boiling water and boil gently until they float to the surface, about 4 minutes. Use a slotted spoon to transfer them to a colander and drain well. Place a few dumplings in each small serving bowl, drizzle with chili garlic oil, and sprinkle with the sesame seeds and scallions.

Use any leftover cabbage to make the noodle salad with salmon skewers on page 135 or the Fruity Slaw on page 163.

PAN-FRIED PORK *and* SHRIMP DUMPLINGS

Makes about 3 dozen

When it's dumpling-making time in my house, it's all hands on deck. After all, if you are going to make dumplings, you might as well make a *ton* of them, because once you get in a groove, they aren't that hard to form and they freeze really well. And hey, isn't that what kids are for? (Kidding, just kidding.) My twins don't exactly love making them, but they love eating them, so with a little gentle coercion, we can bang out a bunch of these in about a half hour. We serve them pan-fried, as here, or in soup (page 127), and they are great either way.

8 ounces large shrimp, peeled and deveined

8 ounces ground pork

2 scallions (green parts only), finely chopped

1 tablespoon soy sauce

1 tablespoon toasted sesame oil

1 tablespoon cornstarch

1 teaspoon grated garlic

1 teaspoon rice vinegar

¼ teaspoon kosher salt

¼ teaspoon sugar

¼ teaspoon ground black pepper

1 package (60-count) round wonton wrappers

2 tablespoons neutral flavored oil

The Very Best Dumpling Sauce (page 41), for serving

Start by making the filling: On a cutting board, use a large chef's knife to finely mince the shrimp nearly to a paste. Transfer the minced shrimp to a large mixing bowl and add the pork, scallions, and the remaining filling ingredients. Mix thoroughly to distribute the seasonings and cornstarch evenly.

To fill the wontons, place a wrapper on your palm and spoon about 1 teaspoon of filling onto the center, avoiding the outer edges. Dip your finger in warm water and run it along the edges of the wrapper to moisten it, then fold the wrapper in half to form a half-moon. Pleat the edges from one end to another, pressing firmly to seal. (If your wontons are not so tidy, don't worry—you will get better with practice. The most important thing is to seal them really well so they don't open up as they cook.)

Place the filled wonton on a baking sheet, press down slightly to flatten its base, and repeat about a million more times, or until you have used up the filling. The wontons are now ready to cook or freeze. If you're freezing them, place them on a baking sheet in the freezer until they're completely firm, then transfer them to a plastic bag. Squeeze out as much air as possible from the bag, then return them to the freezer and store for up to 2 months.

To cook: Coat the bottom of a heavy skillet with a lid with 2 tablespoons of the oil. Add about 20 dumplings to the pan, flat-side down, and cook over medium heat until the oil starts to sizzle, 1 to 2 minutes. Add ¼ cup of water to the pan, cover, and steam the dumplings for 3 minutes, or until the filling is firm and the wrappers are tender. Remove the lid and continue to cook, uncovered, until all the water has evaporated and the bottoms are crisp and golden.

Transfer the fried dumplings to a serving platter and serve with the dipping sauce.

❂ *You can freeze leftover wonton wrappers for a month or two or use them to make Tofu Dumplings (page 97).*

FIRECRACKER SALMON

Serves 4

No one sets out to create a recipe *just* to go viral—who knew when I MacGyver'd this dish to use up some leftover cooked salmon that it would become the recipe I am best known for? But it really does have it all—a blend of crispy, creamy, meaty textures, a bit of heat, and a savory dipping sauce. Many people have told me this dish has become a Friday cocktail-hour tradition, their potluck go-to, and even part of their holiday celebrations, which is just so cool to hear. I've made a bunch of different versions, filling the rice-paper rounds with steak, veggies, or shrimp, but this is the one I keep coming back to. And if you come up with your own variation, don't forget to tag me when you post it!

12 ounces cooked salmon fillet, such as Saucy Sesame Salmon (page 158)

1 large jalapeño pepper, cut in 12 thin slices

4 scallions (green parts only), cut into 2-inch pieces

1 ripe avocado, cut in 12 slices and halved crosswise

12 rice-paper rounds

¼ cup neutral oil, such as avocado or canola

The Very Best Dumpling Sauce (page 41) for dipping

Cut the salmon into twelve equal pieces about 1½ inches square. Arrange the salmon, jalapeño, scallions, and avocado near your work surface. Place the rice-paper rounds and a large, shallow bowl of water next to your work surface. Working with one rice paper at a time, slide each paper quickly into the water, then immediately rotate it through the water to wet the entire surface just until pliable. Shake off the excess water and lay the rice paper on your work surface. Arrange a slice of jalapeño near the bottom of the rice paper and top with 2 pieces of scallion, then 2 slices of avocado. Place a piece of salmon on top. Working quickly but carefully, fold the rice paper away from you to enclose the ingredients, then fold in both sides. Continue to roll the rice paper away from you to form a tidy bundle. Repeat with the remaining ingredients to make 12 bundles.

In a large nonstick skillet, heat 2 tablespoons of the oil over medium-high heat. When a drop of water sizzles in the oil, carefully add 6 of the bundles to the pan folded-side down, and fry until they turn crisp and golden, about 60 seconds. Using tongs, turn the rolls over and brown the second side for a minute or so, then arrange them on a serving plate. Cook the remaining rolls the same way, adding more oil to the skillet if needed. Serve hot with plenty of dumpling sauce for dipping.

Want more ways to use those rice-paper rounds? Make either of the spring roll recipes on page 94.

GOTCHA-GORDON
BELL PEPPER
"SANDWICHES"

page 105

GOTCHA-GORDON BELL PEPPER "SANDWICHES"

Serves 4

A couple of years back, Gordon Ramsay challenged his fans to dream up new sandwich ideas and tag him when they posted them online. I decided to punk him with a keto-friendly version of a turkey and cheese sandwich that substituted slabs of bell pepper for bread, a notion so horrifying to him that he promptly dubbed it an "idiot sandwich." Little did he know that he'd make my carb-free snack an internet sensation. Before you could say BLT, I was appearing on *Good Morning America*, *E! News*, and *The Late Late Show*. Who's the idiot now, Gordon?

Since then I've played around with lots of different fillings and a few of my favorites are below. I find they are an easy after-school snack my girls love, and great in lunchboxes, too. Oh, and Gordon and I have long since buried the hatchet—he's not half as grouchy as he likes people to think!

4 red, yellow, or orange bell peppers
Kosher salt

FILLINGS

The OG

4 ounces low-fat cream cheese (I like the whipped kind for spreading)
¼ cup everything bagel seasoning
12 slices deli-style roast turkey
1 tablespoon yellow or Dijon mustard
1 ounce baby spinach or spring mix

The Cali

1 cup hummus, any flavor (I like roasted garlic)
¼ cup everything bagel seasoning or dukkah
1 hothouse cucumber, thinly sliced
1 tomato, sliced
1 avocado, pitted and sliced
Juice of 1 lemon

Ciao Bella

8 slices prosciutto
4 slices smoked or regular mozzarella
½ cup prepared pesto or good balsamic vinegar
1 peach, sliced (optional but delicious)
2 ounces baby arugula

Cut the peppers in half lengthwise through their stems, and discard the seeds, core, and white ribs.

For each sandwich, layer one-quarter of the fillings into one pepper half in the order listed, making sure to fill the cavity entirely. Top with a second pepper half and press gently with your palm to flatten the sandwich slightly. Serve immediately, or wrap tightly and refrigerate for up to 1 day.

CHICKEN BALT WRAP

Makes 1 big fat wrap, serving 2 as a snack or 1 for lunch

The title's a mouthful and so is this sandwich—it's a definite two-hander! It's also absolutely jam-packed with lean protein, good fats, and zero carbs. Keep everything neat and tidy by packing the filling well and rolling the lettuce tightly. I can't think of a better use for leftover rotisserie chicken, but any kind of cooked poultry and even beef, seafood, or baked tofu make a great wrap. There's no dressing on the filling itself, so do not skip the dipping sauce here.

2 slices turkey bacon, cooked until crisp (see My Tip)

2 large iceberg lettuce leaves from the outer layer

1 carrot, grated

1 cup shredded chicken (I use the breast of a rotisserie chicken)

2 or 3 tomato slices

¼ avocado, sliced

½ cup alfalfa sprouts

Kosher salt and ground black pepper

Green Goddess Dressing (page 139) or store-bought ranch dressing

Air-fry the bacon at 350°F until brown and crisp, about 8 minutes. Pat dry with paper towels and set aside to cool while you assemble the remaining ingredients.

Stack the lettuce leaves with the thicker stem ends toward you. Layer the filling ingredients one at a time starting with the carrot, then the chicken, followed by the bacon, tomato, avocado, and sprouts. Season each layer lightly with salt and pepper as you go.

Bracing the stem ends of the lettuce leaves with your thumbs, use your fingertips to pack the filling ingredients tightly toward you. Roll the stem ends of the lettuce up and over the filling and compact the roll once more. Fold the sides of the lettuce leaves in, burrito-style, and continue rolling the wrap away from you to make a fat, tight cylinder. Place the wrap on a piece of parchment paper and wrap tightly.

Cut the wrap in half and serve to one or two people with a small bowl of dressing for dipping.

My Tip: I always cook my bacon in the air fryer because there is no need to watch or turn it, my stovetop doesn't get splattered with grease, cleanup is minimal, and the strips cook much more evenly than they do in a skillet. Eight minutes works well for regular or turkey bacon; add an extra minute or two if the bacon is thick-cut or if you like it extra crisp.

❋ *Use the rest of the avocado for Firecracker Salmon (page 100) or Avocado Sauce (page 42), or throw it in the freezer for a future Mocha Protein Smoothie (page 54).*

BANH "MY"

Serves 2

Banh My sandwiches are my take on the classic, with lemongrass chicken and pickled veg served in a sweet potato skin instead of the typical baguette. Silly? Sure. Delicious? Definitely! Not only that, it is gluten-free (no bread!) and high in fiber. BTW, having cooked baby sweets in the fridge is a great idea, and not only for making a sammie like this one. Most grocery stores sell net bags of smaller sweet potatoes, which produce perfect single portions. I cook a few whenever I have the oven on and keep them in the fridge to toss into salads or split and broil with some peanut butter as a quickie side (page 210).

2 medium (6- to 8-ounce) sweet potatoes

2 teaspoons neutral oil, such as avocado or canola

¼ cup plain yogurt or Greek yogurt

2 teaspoons sriracha

Pinch of salt

2 Grilled Lemongrass Chicken Thighs (page 170) or other cooked chicken, sliced

1 Persian cucumber, sliced into thin spears

¼ cup Pickled Veggies (page 35)

1 small jalapeño pepper, sliced (optional)

4 cilantro sprigs

Lime wedges

Rub the sweet potatoes lightly with oil and poke in several places with the tines of a fork. Microwave on high until soft, 5 to 6 minutes, depending on the size of your potatoes. When they're cool enough to handle, slit the curved side. Use a spoon to scoop out most of the flesh, creating a pocket. Reserve the flesh for another use (see the ✳ tip).

In a small bowl, stir together the yogurt, sriracha, and salt until smooth.

Stuff the potato skins with the chicken and drizzle with the spicy yogurt. Top with the cucumber, pickled veggies, jalapeño (if using), and cilantro sprigs. Drizzle with a bit more spicy yogurt and serve with a lime wedge for squeezing.

✳ *Save the scooped-out sweet potato flesh for a batch of Thanksgiving Baked Oat Muffins (page 65).*

BROCCA-TUNA MELT

Serves 4 as a snack or 2 for lunch

It's fun to give an old standby like the tuna melt a healthy makeover, especially when the lightened-up version tastes even better than the original! By replacing the mayonnaise with silken tofu, adding raw and cooked broccoli, and topping it all with a modest amount of cheese, I've added protein, slashed the fat, and increased the nutritional value of this diner favorite in one fell swoop. Serving this on rice cakes also makes it gluten-free! If you have leftover cooked broccoli on hand, this is a swell way to use it up—you'll just have a little bit less crunch.

1 small head of broccoli, about 4 ounces

2 (5-ounce) cans tuna, drained

4 ounces silken tofu (about one-quarter of a 14-ounce package)

Juice of ½ lemon

2 tablespoons Dijon mustard

1 teaspoon kosher salt

2 scallions, minced

¼ cup banana pepper rings, optional

8 rice cakes or 4 slices toasted sourdough bread

1 cup shredded Cheddar cheese

Bring a saucepan of salted water to a boil. Separate the florets from the stalk of the broccoli, breaking the head into fairly small pieces. Cook the florets until soft, about 5 minutes. Drain well in a colander.

While the florets cook, peel the broccoli stem, then cut into fine dice. In a mixing bowl, combine the stem and the cooked florets. Use a wooden spoon or a potato masher to crush the florets into small bits.

In the bowl of a food processor, combine the tuna, tofu, lemon juice, mustard, and salt. Process to a smooth puree. Add the scallions and peppers, if using, and pulse once or twice to mince coarsely. Scrape the tuna mixture into the bowl with the broccoli and use a fork to combine well.

Preheat the broiler.

Mound the tuna onto the rice cakes and top evenly with the grated cheese. Broil until the tuna is warmed through and the cheese is melted and starting to brown, about 1 minute. Serve hot.

❄ *Use the rest of the tofu block to make a Mocha Protein Smoothie (page 54) or Chocolate Hazelnut Mousse (page 239).*

Chapter 4

BOWL ME OVER!

Soups, Salads, and
Grain Bowls Galore

IF I HAD TO CHOOSE ONE CHAPTER TO COOK FROM exclusively for the rest of my life, it would probably be this one. I think my family would agree—we are all "soup people" who always seem happiest hunched over a big bowl of something, using our chopsticks, forks, or spoons to compose the perfect bite. And it doesn't begin and end with pho, the aromatic noodle soup that is synonymous with Vietnamese food for many people. As long as it is filled with a mixture of colors, textures, and flavors, a meal in a bowl somehow seems to satisfy my soul as well as my appetite.

Whether the base is broth, grains, or greens, just about all of the dishes you'll find in this chapter qualify as one-pot meals, making them a practical choice when you don't have the bandwidth for a multitude of dishes. This is also a great place to turn if you are someone who, like me, hates letting food go to waste. I consider just about anything in the fridge fair game when it comes to pulling together a salad: last night's steak, the mango that didn't go into my smoothie, some previously cooked noodles, or the stubby end of a cucumber. In fact, just about the only thing you *won't* find in most of these salads and bowls are tender greens that don't hold up well once dressed. That means virtually all the recipes here are great keepers that you can make in quantity and nosh on for several days, and if you are dying for a fix of arugula or butter lettuce, you can use it as a bed for the hardier ingredients when you dish them up.

So go ahead, blitz up a batch of Green Goddess Dressing (page 139) and use it to bring some odds and ends together into a bright, tasty emerald-green salad. Turn that cooked chicken into a soothing soup or put some of last night's sautéed spinach in a good-for-you Buddha Bowl (page 131). Clean out your vegetable bin to make a deeply nourishing soup on a cold day. Nothing goes to waste, no one is the wiser, and you look like a rock star. That's the power of a bowl!

VERY GOOD VEGETABLE BROTH

Makes about 2 quarts

Like everyone else, I resort to broth from a box more than once in a while, but while I have found some brands of chicken broth I like, most store-bought vegetable broth tastes pretty meh to me. Luckily, it's really easy to make a very good vegetable broth, and if you remember to save your kitchen scraps like leek and fennel tops, parsley stems, and even potato and carrot peels, it's also practically free. Just throw this on the back burner while you are making dinner and voilà—you'll get 2 quarts (the equivalent of two 32-ounce boxes) of broth for almost zero effort.

1 tablespoon neutral oil, such as avocado or canola

½ yellow onion or the green tops of 2 leeks, cut into chunks

2 carrots, cut into chunks

2 celery stalks, cut into chunks

1 tablespoon tomato paste

Stalks and leafy fronds from 1 fennel bulb (optional but nice)

4 dried shiitake mushrooms

6 whole peppercorns

1 bay leaf

2 teaspoons kosher salt

In a large soup pot over medium heat, heat the oil until it shimmers. Add the onion, carrots, and celery and sauté until the vegetables start to color a bit, about 6 minutes. Add the tomato paste and stir for 30 seconds, then add the fennel (if using), mushrooms, peppercorns, and bay leaf. Cover with 10 cups of water and bring to a boil, then reduce the heat to low. Simmer partially covered for about 45 minutes. Add the salt.

Place a mesh sieve over a large bowl, pour the broth through the sieve, and discard the solids. Transfer the broth to storage containers. Cool to room temperature and refrigerate for up to 5 days or freeze for up to 3 months.

MY BASIC CHICKEN BROTH

Makes 2 quarts

Making broth from scratch may sound like a lot of trouble when perfectly good broth in boxes (or bouillon paste in jars) can be had. There is no judgment here; as far as I'm concerned, making soup from scratch, even with a few shortcuts, is an accomplishment in its own right. But if you really want to take your soup-making to the next level, or just have delicious, clean, really flavorful broth on hand for stir-fries, rice dishes, and the like, think about making your own once in a while. The work involved is pretty modest for such a big payoff and you can really taste the difference. You'll also get a bonus of cooked chicken meat for salads or soups down the line.

3 chicken leg-thigh quarters (see My Tip)

1 yellow onion, cut into chunks

1 carrot, cut into chunks

2 celery stalks, cut into chunks

1 large plum tomato, coarsely chopped

Stems from 1 bunch cilantro or parsley

2 to 3 teaspoons kosher salt

In a large soup pot, combine the chicken, onion, carrot, celery, tomato, and cilantro stems (don't add the salt yet!). Add 8 cups of water, making sure the ingredients are completely covered, and bring to a boil over medium heat. Immediately reduce the heat to low and skim off any scum floating on the surface. Simmer for 20 minutes.

Using tongs, transfer the chicken to a plate and, when it is cool enough to handle, pull off the meat in big chunks. Return the skin and bones to the pot and continue to simmer, partially covered, for another hour. Add 2 teaspoons of the salt, taste, and add the remaining 1 teaspoon if needed. Place a mesh sieve over a large bowl, pour the broth through the sieve, and discard the solids. Cool to room temperature and skim off as much fat from the surface as you can. Transfer the broth to storage containers and refrigerate for up to 4 days or freeze for up to 3 months. Discard any additional fat that has risen to the top before using.

My Tip: This is a fairly light broth. When I want a deeper chicken flavor, I add the carcass of a rotisserie chicken or extra chicken bones I've saved in a freezer container specifically for broth-making; then I let the broth simmer until it is as flavorful as I want it.

CREAMY ROASTED TOMATO SOUP

Serves 4

It's hard to believe a soup this rich and creamy is actually vegan, but it is! On a rainy day, a piping-hot mugful feels just like a warm hug. It should go without saying that it also makes the perfect companion to a grilled cheese sandwich, made with vegan cheese if you are so inclined. I like to use an immersion blender to puree everything, but a regular blender works fine, too. Just be careful to vent the top to prevent the steam pressure from causing an explosion! This is a very thick soup; if you prefer a thinner consistency, just add a bit more vegetable broth.

⅓ cup raw cashews

4 cups vegetable broth, homemade (page 114) or store-bought

1 pound Campari tomatoes, halved

1 head garlic, top one-third sliced off crosswise to expose the cloves

4 small shallots, peeled

3 tablespoons extra-virgin olive oil, plus more for drizzling

1 teaspoon kosher salt

½ teaspoon ground black pepper

½ teaspoon dried oregano

1 small onion, chopped

2 tablespoons tomato paste

8 basil leaves, plus more for garnish

Fried Shallots (page 33), for garnish (optional)

Preheat the oven to 425°F.

In a glass measuring cup, combine the cashews with 1 cup of the vegetable broth and set aside.

Arrange the tomatoes on a rimmed baking sheet, cut-side up. Nestle the garlic and shallots among the tomatoes. Drizzle with 2 tablespoons of the olive oil, thoroughly coating the cut side of the garlic, and sprinkle with ½ teaspoon of the salt, the pepper, and the oregano. Roast the tomatoes until they have softened and are starting to caramelize a bit, about 30 minutes.

While the tomatoes roast, heat the remaining 1 tablespoon of olive oil in a soup pot over medium heat. When the oil shimmers, add the onions and sauté until they turn translucent, about 5 minutes. Lower the heat to medium-low, add the tomato paste, and stir until it darkens, about 1 minute. Add the remaining 3 cups of vegetable broth and the roasted tomatoes, garlic, and shallots. Use an immersion blender to puree the cashews and their soaking liquid until they turn smooth and creamy. Add the cashews to the pot along with the basil and the remaining ½ teaspoon salt. Puree the soup until smooth.

Reheat the soup if necessary and serve warm, drizzled with a little olive oil and garnished with torn basil leaves and some fried shallots if you like.

✸ *Raw cashews are a godsend when you are avoiding dairy. They make a fantastic whipped cream dupe (page 231) and stand-in for pignolis and cheese in Thai Basil Pesto (page 43), so buy plenty!*

CREAMY ROASTED
TOMATO SOUP

page 116

EASY HOT-*and*-SOUR SOUP

Serves 4 *to* 6

I've always enjoyed the complex yet soothing flavors of hot-and-sour soup, but I never thought much about how full of good protein it is—and how simple it is to make from pantry ingredients. Now it's become one of those "there's nothing to eat in the house" recipes that I turn to when I want something warming and satisfying without a lot of fuss. If you are missing one or two ingredients, NBD, just sub in a texture twin—broccoli stems for the bamboo shoots, julienned zucchini, chicken, or sliced ham for the tofu—or leave it out. There's enough going on here that you won't miss it.

4 cups chicken broth, homemade (page 115) or low-sodium store-bought

1 tablespoon soy sauce

1 tablespoon dark soy sauce

1 teaspoon kosher salt

½ teaspoon red pepper flakes

½ teaspoon ground black pepper

1½ teaspoons sugar

4 ounces fresh shiitake, sliced

1 cup shredded bamboo shoots

8 ounces firm tofu, sliced and cut into strips

2 tablespoons toasted sesame oil

1 tablespoon cornstarch mixed with 1 tablespoon cold water

3 eggs, lightly beaten

2 tablespoons distilled white vinegar, or to taste

3 scallions (white and green parts), thinly sliced, for serving

In a large saucepan, bring the chicken broth to a simmer over medium-high heat. Season with both of the soy sauces, salt, red pepper flakes, black pepper, and sugar. Then add the mushrooms, bamboo shoots, tofu, and sesame oil and bring to a simmer.

Stir in the cornstarch mixture and cook until the soup thickens, 1 or 2 minutes. Give the soup a good stir and gradually pour the beaten eggs into the swirling broth. Cook the eggs without stirring until just set, about 1 minute, then stir well to distribute the egg shreds. Stir in the vinegar, adding a bit more if you like it tangier. Ladle the soup into bowls and serve, sprinkled with the scallions.

✿ *Even if you buy a small can of bamboo shoots, you are likely to have leftovers. Add them to a Buddha Bowl (page 131), or toss them into a stir-fry like the Chicken-Veggie Pan Fry with Glass Noodles (page 155).*

CURRIED CAULIFLOWER *and* RED LENTIL SOUP

Serves 4

Ready in just about 30 minutes, this soup gets a lot of earthy flavor and a bit of gentle heat from Thai red curry paste. The red lentils break down so completely that you won't even know they are there, but they give the soup body and some extra protein. This is another soup that can easily be made vegan if you are having a meatless day. Don't skip the fried shallots—they add crunch and are just so delicious.

1 tablespoon neutral oil, such as avocado or canola

½ large yellow onion, chopped

1½ teaspoons kosher salt

2 garlic cloves, minced

2 tablespoons Thai red curry paste

1 pound cauliflower (about ½ head), chopped

¾ cup red lentils

4 cups chicken or vegetable broth, homemade (page 115 or 114) or store-bought, or water

½ cup full-fat coconut milk

Juice of 1 lime, or to taste

Fried Shallots (page 33), for garnish

Chopped fresh cilantro, for garnish

Heat the oil in a large saucepan or soup pot over medium heat. Add the onion and ½ teaspoon of the salt and cook, stirring, until it starts to soften, about 4 minutes. Add the garlic and curry paste and stir until fragrant, 1 or 2 minutes. Add the cauliflower, lentils, the remaining 1 teaspoon of salt, and broth to the pot. Bring to a boil, then reduce the heat to low and simmer, covered, for 20 minutes. The cauliflower and lentils should be very tender.

Use an immersion blender to puree the soup until very smooth. (Alternatively, transfer to a blender and puree, being sure to vent the top as you blend; return the soup to the pot.) Stir in the coconut milk and lime juice and reheat if necessary, adding a bit of water if the soup is too thick. Serve hot, garnished with a sprinkle of fried shallots and chopped cilantro.

Use the rest of the cauliflower head to make a Chili Beef Skillet Dinner (page 179) or Furikake Potato Salad (page 192), or add it to the roast veggies in the Sheet-Pan Five-Spice Chicken Legs with Squash and Broccolini (page 167).

WELLNESS SOUP

Serves 4

When you are feeling under the weather, chicken soup is nearly always the best medicine—especially when it's made with as many restorative ingredients as this sunny bowlful. It's brothy because you need plenty of liquids when you are sick, it's garlicky because garlic is good for what ails you, and the slippery glass noodles are easy on a sore throat. Best of all, it's so easy to make that you can be back under the covers with a steaming mug in about 20 minutes.

1 tablespoon avocado oil

½ onion, chopped

6 garlic cloves, minced

1½ teaspoons kosher salt

2 tablespoons Solid-Gold Turmeric Paste (page 29)

1 small (4- to 6-ounce) sweet potato, peeled and cubed

½ teaspoon ground black pepper

4 cups chicken broth, homemade (page 115) or store-bought

3 ounces glass noodles

4 small heads baby bok choy, sliced crosswise, or any other green veggie like chard, green beans, or spinach

1½ cups shredded cooked chicken

Heat the oil in a soup pot over medium heat. When the oil shimmers, add the onion, garlic, and ½ teaspoon of the salt and sauté until the onion has softened, about 3 minutes. Add the turmeric paste and stir to coat everything, then add the sweet potato, pepper, chicken broth, and the remaining 1 teaspoon of salt. Raise the heat to medium-high and bring to a boil, then reduce the heat to low and simmer until the sweet potato is tender, about 8 minutes.

While the sweet potato simmers, bring a large saucepan of water to a boil. Add the noodles and cook until they are just al dente, about 4 minutes. Drain the noodles in a colander.

Stir the bok choy and chicken into the simmering soup and cook until the chicken is warmed through and the bok choy is wilted. Stir in the noodles, heat through, and serve hot.

THE ESSENTIAL CHICKEN PHO

Serves 4

Left to my own devices, I will make pho from just about anything: oxtail, half a rotisserie chicken, even the carcass of our Thanksgiving turkey. All of them are delicious, but this is the one my girls request when they are feeling under the weather, homesick, or, you know, hungry. In other words, they would eat it every day if they could! I've added some green vegetables and quail eggs to make this a really special bowlful, but they are totally optional. If you are pressed for time, this can simmer for as little as 30 minutes; after 45, though, the flavor will be deeper and more developed. Bring the steaming bowls to the table and let everyone doctor their own bowls with their condiments and toppings of choice.

2 to 3 ounces fresh ginger, peeled and cut into chunks

2 small white onions, halved

3 meaty chicken leg-thigh quarters

1 tablespoon fish sauce

1 ounce rock sugar or 1 tablespoon granulated sugar

1 teaspoon kosher salt

1 Pho Spice Sachet (page 28)

4 ounces rice noodles, fresh or dried (see My Tip)

2 cups green vegetables, such as broccoli florets, Chinese broccoli (gai lan), or bok choy, cut into bite-size pieces

1 (15-ounce) can cooked quail eggs, halved (optional)

FOR SERVING

4 large sprigs Thai basil or ¼ cup chopped cilantro

2 cups bean sprouts

1 lemon or lime, cut into 8 wedges

1 large jalapeño pepper, sliced (optional)

Sriracha or chili oil

Hoisin sauce

Place a soup pot over medium-high heat and add the ginger and onions, cut-side down. Sear them without moving until they begin to char, about 6 minutes. Add the chicken to the pot and enough cold water to cover completely.

Stir in the fish sauce, sugar, and salt. Add the spice sachet to the pot. Bring to a boil, then reduce the heat to low and simmer for 30 to 45 minutes, skimming the surface of the broth once or twice to remove any foam that floats to the top. Transfer the chicken to a plate and, when it is cool enough to handle, shred the meat, discarding the skin and bones.

Taste the broth for seasoning, adding more salt or fish sauce if needed. Strain the broth into a large bowl, discard the solids, and return the broth to the pot.

Bring a large pot of water to a boil. Add the rice noodles and cook for about 45 seconds, or according to the package directions. Use tongs to transfer the noodles to a colander and drain.

In the same pot, cook your vegetables until they turn bright green and just tender, about 3 minutes, depending on the thickness and size of the pieces. Drain well in a colander.

To serve, reheat the broth if necessary to a low boil. Divide the noodles among four serving bowls and top each one with some of the vegetables and shredded chicken. Ladle the boiling-hot broth over each portion and serve with the herbs, toppings, and condiments.

My Tip: Fresh rice noodles, which I prefer, take just seconds to heat through; if you are using dried noodles, they will take between 1 and 3 minutes to soften. Just keep sampling them until they have the texture you want.

✻ *Don't let the extra Thai basil wilt and die; make a batch of Thai Basil Pesto (page 43) while the broth simmers, or make Eggplant and Tofu Stir-Fry (page 156).*

WONTON SOUP *with* BOK CHOY

Serves 4

There is something so soothing about an old-school bowl of wonton soup, and when it's made with your own homemade dumplings it's just that much better. I like to add some vegetables and mushrooms to make the broth even more savory, plus a generous drizzle of chili garlic oil. For those with really hearty appetites, add some cooked wheat noodles to the bowl for a real Chinatown-style treat.

2 dozen Pork and Shrimp Dumplings (page 98) or Tofu Dumplings (page 97)

6 cups chicken broth, homemade (page 115) or store-bought

1 tablespoon soy sauce

2 teaspoons chicken or mushroom bouillon powder (optional)

1 teaspoon toasted sesame oil, or to taste

4 heads baby bok choy, leaves separated

6 fresh shiitake mushrooms, stems removed, and sliced

Chili Garlic Oil (page 38), for serving

Bring a large pot of water to a boil. Add 12 wontons to the boiling water and cook until they float to the surface, about 4 minutes. Use a skimmer or a slotted spoon to scoop the wontons into a colander, then repeat with an additional twelve wontons.

In a large, deep saucepan, bring the chicken broth to a low boil over medium heat. Add the soy sauce, bouillon powder (if using), and sesame oil. Add the bok choy and mushrooms and cook until the greens are just wilted and still bright green, 2 to 3 minutes. Add the wontons to the pot and boil for 30 seconds or so to heat through.

Ladle the soup and wontons into bowls, drizzle with chili garlic oil to taste, and serve hot.

TAMARIND SOUP *with* SALMON, TOMATOES, *and* PINEAPPLE

Serves 4

You know those recipes that are so much more than just the sum of their parts? This is a perfect example, and a quick skim of the ingredients list can't really convey the complex interplay of tart, tangy, bright, and sweet you get in each bite. It's hard to believe a soup this flavorful can be made with water, but trust me, the tamarind gives it a surprising amount of body and depth. Omit the okra (or substitute green beans) if you must, but when cooked quickly as it is here, the okra is crunchy and fresh, not stringy and gooey. Try it, you might like it! Serve this over a small scoop of rice for a complete and completely satisfying meal.

1 pound salmon fillets

1½ teaspoons kosher salt

¼ teaspoon ground black pepper

1 scallion (white and green parts), chopped

1 tablespoon fish sauce

1 cup pineapple chunks, preferably fresh

½ small onion, quartered and separated into a few pieces

2 plum tomatoes, cut into large chunks

1½ ounces tamarind pulp (see My Tip)

½ cup small broccoli florets

8 small okra pods, cut into ½-inch pieces

2 red Thai chiles

¼ cup chopped fresh cilantro, plus more for garnish

2 cups cooked rice, for serving

Pat the salmon fillets dry and sprinkle with ½ teaspoon of the salt, the pepper, and the scallions. Set aside.

Bring 5 cups of water to a boil in a soup pot and season with the remaining 1 teaspoon of salt and the fish sauce. Add the pineapple, onion, tomatoes, tamarind pulp, and salmon fillets, and bring to a gentle boil. Reduce the heat to medium-low and simmer for 4 minutes, making sure the salmon is submerged in the liquid.

Add the broccoli, okra, whole chiles, and cilantro, and cook until the salmon is cooked through and the broccoli is tender-crisp, about 4 minutes.

To serve, place a scoop of rice in each serving bowl. Break the salmon into bite-size pieces, discard the skin, and return it to the pot. Ladle the hot soup over the rice and garnish with a bit more cilantro.

My Tip: If you can't find tamarind pulp, use concentrate or powder and follow the substitution recommendations on the package. You want the soup tart but not so heavily flavored that it overwhelms the salmon. Start with just a little and add more as needed as the soup cooks.

✻ *Fresh pineapple is a great addition to coleslaw (page 163), and it perks up Flash-Fried Flounder with Quick Pineapple Salsa (page 161), so don't hesitate to buy a whole fruit.*

BUDDHA BOWL

Serves 2

I can't count how many times I've grabbed a Buddha bowl at a juice bar or an airport takeout spot because it seemed like the healthiest option, only to find myself looking at a big bowl of rice with just a few veggies sprinkled on top. That is definitely not the case with my version, which ditches the rice for a lighter base of cabbage and quinoa and piles on substantial toppings like tofu, peppers, and edamame for plenty of protein, crunch, and staying power.

⅓ cup raw quinoa (the red or brown varieties look prettiest here)

½ teaspoon kosher salt

3 cups shredded green or purple cabbage (about one-quarter of a small cabbage)

8 ounces firm or extra-firm tofu, patted dry and cut into ½-inch cubes

½ teaspoon My Spice Blend (page 29)

¼ teaspoon Chinese five-spice powder

Avocado oil cooking spray

¼ cup Tamarind Ketchup (page 36)

2 tablespoons neutral oil, such as avocado or canola

1 cup frozen shelled edamame, thawed

1 small carrot, shredded

1 red or yellow bell pepper, cored and thinly sliced

½ avocado, diced

½ cup Pickled Veggies (page 35)

½ cup steamed spinach or broccoli

2 tablespoons furikake, homemade (page 32) or store-bought, or finely shredded seaweed, for garnish

In a small saucepan, combine the quinoa with ⅔ cup of water and the salt and bring to a boil over high heat. Reduce the heat to low, cover, and simmer until the water is absorbed and the quinoa's curly white tails are visible, about 12 minutes. Let the quinoa stand, covered, for 5 minutes, then transfer to a large bowl. Add the cabbage and toss to combine; the cabbage should soften and wilt just a bit. Set aside.

Preheat your air fryer to 400°F. Meanwhile, spread the tofu cubes on a kitchen towel and top with a second towel. Press lightly to absorb some of the moisture. Transfer the cubes to a bowl and sprinkle with the spice blend and five-spice powder. Toss to coat the cubes evenly, spray with the avocado oil cooking spray, and toss again.

Air-fry the tofu cubes for 5 minutes, then toss and air-fry again until they start to crisp at the edges, about another 5 minutes.

In a small bowl, mix the tamarind ketchup with the oil and 2 tablespoons of water.

Divide the cabbage-quinoa mixture between two deep bowls and top with the tofu. Arrange small piles of edamame, carrot, pepper, avocado, pickled vegetables, and spinach around the tofu and drizzle with the tamarind dressing. Garnish with the furikake and serve.

✻ *Use the rest of the frozen edamame in a Chicken Salad with Mandarin Oranges (page 141), or add them to any of the stir-fries or fried rice recipes for a bit of extra protein.*

VERMICELLI BOWLS *with* GRILLED SHRIMP *and* PICKLED VEGGIES

Serves 4

You'll find this at any Vietnamese restaurant worth its salt because it's a classic. It's a great example of meals that are really speedy to put together if you have taken the time to stock up on a few of my most-used homemade condiments, like Nuoc Cham, Pickled Veggies, and Lemongrass Shallot Paste. If you haven't, though, don't let that deter you—you can put them all together from scratch (or substitute chopped fresh lemongrass) and still have this on the table in about 30 minutes. I use extra-large shrimp because the smaller ones are easier to overcook, but either size works in this recipe. Just reduce the cooking time a bit and keep an eye on the skewers as they grill to prevent your shrimp from drying out.

1 pound extra-large shrimp, peeled and deveined

1 tablespoon Lemongrass Shallot Paste (page 30) or ½ tablespoon finely minced fresh lemongrass and 1 small shallot, minced

¼ teaspoon kosher salt

¼ teaspoon ground black pepper

4 ounces rice vermicelli noodles

Avocado oil cooking spray

FOR SERVING

1 cup bean sprouts

1 Persian cucumber, thinly sliced

1 cup Pickled Veggies (page 35)

½ cup lightly crushed raw peanuts

1 red Thai chile or Fresno chile, thinly sliced

1 cup Nuoc Cham (page 39)

4 mint sprigs

4 cilantro sprigs

Combine the shrimp and lemongrass paste in a large bowl and toss to coat the shrimp evenly. Season with the salt and pepper and toss again. Set aside.

Bring a large pot of water to a boil over medium-high heat. Add the noodles and cook until just al dente; do not overcook, or your dish will be too sticky. Drain well and set aside.

Preheat your air fryer to 350°F. Thread the shrimp onto wooden skewers, four per skewer, and spray them lightly on both sides with avocado oil cooking spray. Arrange the skewers in the air fryer in a single layer and cook for 3 minutes. Flip the skewers and cook until the shrimp are browned on the edges and just cooked through, another 3 to 5 minutes.

To serve, divide the noodles among four deep bowls. Top each serving with the bean sprouts, cucumber, and pickled veggies. Place a shrimp skewer on top of each serving, sprinkle with the peanuts, and drizzle the nuoc cham over all. Top with the herb sprigs and serve.

✽ *Save the extra peanuts for a Tin Roof Parfait (page 227) or sprinkle them on the Grilled Salmon Skewers on Tangy Noodle Salad (page 135).*

GRILLED SALMON SKEWERS *on* TANGY NOODLE SALAD

Serves 6

Don't take my word that this recipe rocks—it won the summer cookout challenge when I made it on *LIVE with Kelly and Ryan*! The sweet-salty-sour grilling glaze does double duty as a dressing for the noodle and veggie base, so it comes together really quickly. I grilled the shrimp on a barbecue, but a ridged grill pan will work just fine and you won't even need to wait for a sunny day.

SALAD
4 cups shredded purple cabbage, about ¼ of a head

2 large carrots, peeled and shredded

1 red bell pepper, cored, seeded, and thinly sliced

2 Persian cucumbers, cut into thin strips

½ cup lightly packed fresh mint leaves

1 cup cooked soba noodles

MARINADE-DRESSING
2 tablespoons soy sauce

2 tablespoons toasted sesame oil

1 tablespoon black vinegar

1 tablespoon brown sugar

¼ teaspoon kosher salt

¼ teaspoon ground black pepper

1 bunch (about 6) scallions

1½ pounds thick salmon fillets

½ fresh pineapple

Avocado oil cooking spray

¼ cup fresh orange juice

1 tablespoon sesame seeds

In a large bowl, combine the cabbage, carrots, bell peppers, cucumbers, mint, and soba noodles, and set aside.

To make the marinade-dressing: In a large measuring cup, combine the soy sauce, sesame oil, black vinegar, brown sugar, salt, and pepper. Thinly slice two of the scallions and add them to the bowl; cut the rest into 2-inch pieces.

Cut the salmon into 2-inch cubes and place in a large bowl. Slice the rind off the pineapple with a sharp knife, then cut the flesh into chunks similar in size to the salmon cubes and add to the bowl. Pour half of the soy sauce marinade over the salmon and pineapple chunks, and turn the fish pieces to coat them evenly. Thread the salmon and pineapple chunks onto six metal or wooden skewers, alternating with the scallion pieces. Reserve any marinade left in the bowl.

Preheat a ridged grill pan or a barbecue grill until it turns medium-hot. Spray the skewers with a little avocado oil cooking spray. Grill the salmon skewers for about 6 minutes total, turning them frequently to brown all over and brushing each just-grilled side with the marinade left in the marinating bowl. Transfer the skewers to a plate and keep warm.

Add the orange juice to the reserved soy mixture in the measuring cup and stir. Pour the dressing over the salad and toss to coat evenly. Divide the salad among six serving bowls and top each one with a salmon skewer. Sprinkle with the sesame seeds and serve.

❉ *Finish off the rest of the cabbage in the Fruity Slaw (page 163) or the Buddha Bowl (page 131).*

GREEK SALAD
with SHRIMP
and ARTICHOKES

page 138

GREEK SALAD *with* SHRIMP *and* ARTICHOKES

Serves 4 to 6

Everyone's favorite side salad becomes a satisfying main course meal when you add some additional protein in the form of beans, shrimp, and just enough quinoa to soak up all those delicious juices. Some sliced artichoke hearts (I like the jarred ones in brine, not oil) give this good-looking salad even more flavor and texture, although if you don't have any on hand, it's not a deal-breaker—there is plenty going on in this bowl either way. This is a great keeper, perfect for pack-along lunches or ready-to-go dinners when you get home late and don't feel like cooking. Resist the urge to overdress the salad; the veggies will produce some juices (and dilute the sharp dressing) as the salad sits.

8 ounces large shrimp, peeled and deveined

1 lemon, sliced

½ teaspoon kosher salt

1 cup cooked quinoa

1 (15-ounce) can cannellini beans, drained

1 cup artichoke hearts, quartered

1 pint cherry tomatoes, halved

½ cup pitted kalamata olives, halved

4 Persian cucumbers or 2 regular cucumbers, halved, seeded, and cut into bite-size pieces

4 ounces feta cheese, cubed

2 tablespoons capers, drained

½ small red onion, thinly sliced

RED WINE VINAIGRETTE

2 tablespoons fresh lemon juice

1 tablespoon red wine vinegar

1½ teaspoons za'atar or dried oregano

1 teaspoon kosher salt

½ teaspoon ground black pepper

⅓ cup extra-virgin olive oil

In a medium pot, bring 4 cups of water to a boil. Place the shrimp and lemon slices in a large heatproof bowl, add the salt, and cover with the boiling water. Cover the bowl with a plate and set aside for 10 minutes to cook the shrimp.

Drain the shrimp and return them to the bowl. Add the remaining salad ingredients and toss gently to distribute the quinoa and capers.

In a small bowl, stir together the lemon juice, vinegar, za'atar, salt, and pepper. Whisk in the olive oil in a steady stream until everything is well combined and emulsified.

Pour half of the vinaigrette over the salad and mix gently; you don't want to break up the feta too much. If the salad looks too dry, add more dressing a tablespoon at a time, just until the ingredients are lightly coated.

The salad tastes best when allowed to stand for at least 30 minutes for the flavors to mingle.

❋ *If you have extra feta, add it to some Grab-and-Go Egg Jars (page 59).*

138

GREEN GODDESS CHICKEN CHOPPED SALAD

Serves 4

Crunchy, savory, and full of protein and healthy fats, this salad is as green as they come. It's all about the creamy, bright dressing, a lightened-up version of the traditional green goddess that gets its special depth of flavor from—shhh!—a couple of anchovies. This recipe makes a generous amount of dressing, and you will find all sorts of ways to use the leftovers; it's perfect on broiled salmon, as a dip for cooked shrimp, or mixed into egg yolks for a delicious deviled egg filling.

GREEN GODDESS DRESSING

½ cup fresh baby spinach

¼ cup chopped chives or scallion tops

1 cup fresh green herbs, such as parsley, dill, basil, and mint (I like ¼ cup of each)

2 anchovies

1 garlic clove

¼ cup plain yogurt

2 tablespoons Kewpie mayonnaise

3 tablespoons fresh lemon juice

¼ cup avocado oil

3 cups chopped cooked chicken (see sidebar), cut into small dice

1 small head romaine lettuce, chopped

1 small or ½ large fennel bulb, trimmed and chopped

2 firm avocados, cut into small dice

3 scallions (white and green parts)

Flatbread crackers or endive spears, for serving

Combine the dressing ingredients in a small blender or food processor and blitz until the herbs are finely chopped and the dressing is bright green. Set aside.

In a mixing bowl, combine the chicken, lettuce, fennel, avocado, and scallions.

Drizzle about ¾ cup of the dressing over the salad and toss to combine; add a bit more if the salad looks too dry.

Serve with flatbread crackers or endive spears for scooping.

Perfect Air-Fryer Chicken Breasts

Skip the cooked chicken strips you can buy at the grocery store; nine times out of ten, they are dry and full of preservatives. Cooking boneless, skinless breasts in the air fryer is nearly as convenient (just toss them in while you are doing other kitchen tasks), and you'll have much juicier, tastier meat at half the cost. Rub two good-sized breasts (about 12 ounces each) with a bit of olive oil and season them liberally on both sides with My Spice Blend (page 29). Cook the breasts in a preheated 400°F air fryer for 10 minutes, turning after 5 minutes. The internal temperature should be 160°F; if not, cook for an additional minute. Let the breasts rest for 5 minutes before slicing or cubing, or cool to room temperature and refrigerate whole (they will dry out more quickly if cut up). They will keep in the refrigerator for up to 3 days or up to 3 months in the freezer.

CHICKEN SALAD
with MANDARIN ORANGES

Serves 4

Sometimes things are so out they are in, and that just might be the case with this salad. It's an obvious throwback to the "Chinese" chicken salads of the last century (minus the chow mein noodles, thank you very much). But I still find the combination of those mandarin orange segments with the creamy dressing irresistible, and with chicken and edamame, this salad has plenty of nutrients in every bite.

3 cups shredded cooked chicken (see Perfect Air-Fryer Chicken Breasts, page 139, or use the breast of a rotisserie chicken)

3 cups baby kale (about half of a 5-ounce package) or baby arugula

2 cups bean sprouts

1 cup frozen shelled edamame, thawed

1 carrot, shaved with a vegetable peeler or shredded

3 scallions, thinly sliced

1 cup mandarin orange segments (about 2 mandarin oranges)

½ cup Pickled Veggies (page 35)

DRESSING

¼ cup smooth peanut butter

3 tablespoons rice vinegar

1 tablespoon toasted sesame oil

1 tablespoon honey

2 teaspoons soy sauce

Ground black pepper

½ cup chopped roasted almonds

In a large bowl, combine the chicken, kale, bean sprouts, edamame, carrot, scallions, oranges, and pickled veggies, and toss to combine.

To make the dressing: In a measuring cup, combine the peanut butter, rice vinegar, sesame oil, honey, soy sauce, and pepper with 2 tablespoons of water and whisk until smooth. Divide the salad among four serving plates and drizzle with the dressing. Sprinkle with the chopped almonds and serve with more dressing at the table.

✳ *Drizzle any leftover orange segments in Spiced Orange Caramel Sauce (page 218) and top with grated chocolate for a simple dessert.*

HOLD-*the*-BUN CHEESEBURGER SALAD

Serves 4

You get all the satisfaction of a big cheesy burger from this salad with many more healthy greens (and a lot less overprocessed bun and carbs!). I like to cook the beef smashburger-style to get all those browned, tasty bits, but if you prefer to sauté the ground beef into crumbles and top the salad with shredded cheese, that works, too. The bacon is optional, but don't skip the Cheddar crisps—they are addictively crunchy.

8 ounces sharp Cheddar cheese, grated

1 pound lean ground beef

Kosher salt and ground black pepper

"SPECIAL SAUCE" DRESSING

½ cup plain Greek yogurt

2 tablespoons ketchup

2 tablespoons gochujang or sriracha

1 tablespoon pickle relish with its juice

1 tablespoon yellow or Dijon mustard

Kosher salt

FOR SERVING

6 cups (about 4 ounces) baby kale and spinach blend or other greens

1 large tomato, chopped

Sliced cucumbers, pickle chips, pickled red onions, sliced banana peppers, or other burger toppings of your choice

Place a large nonstick skillet over medium heat. Use half of the grated cheese to make four compact mounds in the skillet, leaving enough room between them so the cheese can spread out as it melts (you may need to do this in two batches). When the cheese has melted and is turning brown at the edges, about 3 minutes, carefully flip the crisps and brown the other side for 1 more minute. Transfer to a plate.

Divide the beef into four equal portions and form each one into a ball. Season with salt and pepper. Place the same skillet you used for the cheese crisps over medium-high heat. When the pan is hot, add two of the beef balls and cook until they're very well browned on the underside, about 4 minutes. Flip the balls seared-side up and, with a wide metal spatula, press down on them firmly, spreading them to about ¼ inch in thickness. Cook until they're browned, about 2 minutes. Then flip the burgers again, top each one with one-quarter of the remaining grated cheese, and cover the pan. Cook until the cheese has melted and the burgers are browned and crispy at the edges, about another 2 minutes. Transfer to a plate and repeat with the remaining beef and cheese.

To make the "special sauce" dressing: Combine all the ingredients in a bowl or small blender. Stir or blend thoroughly.

To serve, arrange the greens and tomatoes in four serving bowls and top with a cheeseburger, breaking each burger into bite-size pieces. Sprinkle with any additional toppings you prefer, and drizzle with the "special sauce." Crumble a cheese crisp over each serving and enjoy.

STEAK SALAD *with* CREAMY CHIMICHURRI

Serves 4 generously

Composed salads like Cobb or tuna niçoise always look a little more elegant than a mixed salad, and this one boasts so much texture, color, and protein that it will win over even the most confirmed carnivore. The herby dressing has a little kick and a *ton* of flavor, so double up and use the leftovers on grilled chicken or fish, or as a sandwich spread. If you have leftover roast lamb, this would be a great way to repurpose it, too.

CHIMICHURRI

2 cups fresh parsley, cilantro, or mint, or a combination

2 scallions (white and green parts), chopped

3 garlic cloves, chopped

1 small jalapeño pepper, seeded and diced

3 tablespoons red wine vinegar

Juice of 1 lime

1 teaspoon kosher salt

¼ teaspoon ground black pepper

⅓ cup olive oil

¼ cup crumbled feta cheese

4 large eggs

6 small red or Yukon Gold potatoes, quartered

6 ounces green beans, trimmed

1 small head romaine lettuce, chopped

8 ounces cooked steak or lamb

1 (15.5-ounce) can black beans, drained

1 avocado, sliced

1 pint grape or cherry tomatoes, halved

½ red onion, thinly sliced

To make the chimichurri: Place the herbs, scallions, garlic, jalapeño, vinegar, and lime juice in a blender and blend until the herbs and vegetables are finely chopped but not pureed. Season with salt and pepper. Then, with the blender running, stream in the olive oil until blended. Add the feta and blend just until combined and creamy. Set the chimichurri aside to allow the flavors to mingle while you assemble the salad.

Place the eggs and potatoes in a deep pot with enough water to cover. Bring to a boil over medium-high heat, reduce the heat to low, and simmer for 8 minutes. With a slotted spoon, transfer the eggs to a bowl of cold water and add the green beans to the pot with the potatoes. Continue to cook until the beans and potatoes are tender, about 4 minutes. Drain them in a colander.

Spread the romaine lettuce on a large serving platter and arrange the green beans, potatoes, steak, black beans, avocado, and tomatoes on top in neat rows. Peel and halve the eggs and arrange them around the edges, then sprinkle with the red onions. Drizzle with the chimichurri and serve.

Chapter 5

DINNER'S READY

From Weeknight Warriors to Weekend Wows

IN THE TRADITIONAL VIETNAMESE HOUSEHOLD where I grew up, dinner was always a multicourse event. It started with soup, then a fish dish, then a stir-fry—just a nonstop parade of dishes. It was amazing, but so was the sink full of dishes these meals left in their wake. My approach to dinner is the complete opposite of my parents'. I keep it simple but full of flavor, and if it can all be cooked in one pot or on a sheet pan, so much the better.

Over time, I've developed a roster of proven crowd-pleasers that I know will make everyone happy, including the cook. With multiple picky eaters to feed—and that most definitely includes my husband—I've learned the hard way that mealtimes go more smoothly when I don't try to nudge anyone *too* far outside of their comfort zone. Not surprisingly, chicken, salmon, shrimp, and the occasional beef or pork dish are in most frequent rotation.

Most of these weeknight dinners feature reasonable portions of lean protein, a supersized serving of veggies, and a few carbs to round things out. More often than not, it's rice, since that's the one starch I know everyone in my family will eat. I generally stick to protein and veggies and keep my portion of rice, noodles, or potatoes to around half a cup while my family gets more generous servings. That way, we can all eat together without too many compromises or a lot of extra effort. I'll leave it to you to decide how much you want on your plate, but I promise that even if you go easy on the carbs as I do, you'll find these meals are completely satisfying.

One final note: Don't feel you need to restrict yourself to the options in this chapter when five o'clock rolls around. My family is happy with a big bowl of soup or a hearty, protein-powered salad for dinner, and yours will be, too. As long as you are making sure everyone has their nutritional bases covered, you have hit a home run. So, break out some real napkins and place mats, maybe add one of the treats in Chapter 7 to the menu, and enjoy the best time of the day, every day.

SHRIMP SUSHI BAKE

Serves 4

I love to take trends that blow up online and push them to the next level, and this sushi bake that broke the internet—a layered casserole of seasoned rice, seafood, and plenty of toppings—is a perfect example. I season both the rice and the shrimp to give them more oomph, add a hint of creaminess, and top half of the pan with avocado (just half, because not everyone is a fan of warm avocado). I use roasted seaweed snacks for my wrappers because they are the perfect size for scooping up a bite of rice and topping, but if you have nori sheets on hand, cutting them into 3 × 4-inch strips is much more economical. Leftover rice is fine for this, but if it's coming straight from the fridge, warming it in the microwave for 30 seconds will make it easier to incorporate the seasonings.

Avocado oil cooking spray

8 ounces large shrimp, peeled and deveined

2 scallions (white and green parts), minced

2 ounces cream cheese, at room temperature

¼ cup Kewpie mayonnaise (see My Tip), plus more for garnish

1 teaspoon soy sauce

½ teaspoon kosher salt

4 cups cooked short-grain or jasmine rice

2 tablespoons mirin

2 tablespoons rice vinegar

1 tablespoon toasted sesame oil

½ cup furikake, homemade (page 32) or store-bought

1 avocado, sliced

Sriracha, homemade (page 36) or store-bought, for garnish

Nori sheets or seaweed snacks, for serving

Preheat the oven to 350°F. Lightly spray a 9 × 9-inch square baking dish with the avocado oil cooking spray.

Use a large chef's knife to finely mince the shrimp (you can also pulse the shrimp in a food processor if you prefer, but don't puree it to a paste). In a medium bowl, combine the minced shrimp, scallions, cream cheese, Kewpie mayo, soy sauce, and salt and mix thoroughly.

Add the rice to the baking dish and sprinkle with the mirin, rice vinegar, sesame oil, and all but 2 tablespoons of the furikake. Mix well with a fork to distribute the seasonings, then pat the rice down into an even layer—you don't need to press it too firmly. Spread the shrimp mixture evenly over the rice and dust with the remaining 2 tablespoons of furikake. Arrange the avocado slices over half of the pan. Decorate the top with diagonal lines of mayo crisscrossed with diagonal lines of sriracha.

Bake until the shrimp is fully cooked and starting to brown around the edges, about 20 minutes.

Let cool for 5 minutes, then place the baking dish in the center of the table and serve with the nori sheets.

My Tip: If you don't have Kewpie or another Japanese-style squirtable mayo, you can make your own by thinning down regular mayonnaise with a little fresh lemon juice and a teeny bit of agave nectar or maple syrup, then transfer to a squeeze bottle.

✳ *Shred extra nori sheets onto your Buddha Bowl (page 131), or make a batch of furikake (page 32).*

ORZOTTO *with* SHRIMP *and* ASPARAGUS

Serves 4

If you love risotto but hate the constant stirring, this dish will make your day. Rice-shaped orzo pasta stands in for the rice, and as it cooks and absorbs the broth, it becomes super silky and soft with minimal stirring. I like the way this looks with a mix of spring veggies, but you can stick to one or two types if you want; just make sure the total quantity is about 2 cups. The shrimp and peas can go into the pan directly from the freezer, making this a great last-minute pantry meal.

1 tablespoon unsalted butter

1 small shallot, minced

⅔ cup orzo

1⅓ cups chicken or vegetable broth, homemade (page 115 or 114) or store-bought

Zest and juice of 1 lemon

¼ teaspoon kosher salt

1 pound large shrimp, peeled and deveined

¾ cup asparagus pieces

¾ cup sugar snap peas, trimmed

½ cup frozen peas

2 tablespoons chopped fresh dill

1 tablespoon chopped fresh chives

Melt the butter in a deep skillet over medium heat. Add the shallot and sauté until translucent, 2 to 3 minutes. Add the orzo and toast, stirring often, until the grains are golden and slightly browned, 3 or 4 minutes. Add the broth, lemon juice, and salt and bring to a simmer. Cover and cook for 8 minutes, stirring once or twice to make sure the orzo is not sticking.

Add the shrimp to the pan in a single layer, cover, and cook for 2 minutes. Uncover the pan and arrange the asparagus, sugar snap peas, and frozen peas on top of the shrimp (see My Tip). Cover the pan and cook for 6 minutes longer.

Stir in the lemon zest, dill, and chives. Taste and add more lemon juice and salt if needed. Serve immediately.

My Tip: Cooking the vegetables along with the orzo is convenient, but it will inevitably cause some of their brightness to fade. If you want the veggies to stay at their most vibrant, blanch them briefly in boiling water, rinse them under cold water to set the color, and then cook them with the pasta and shrimp just long enough to heat through.

Don't let your leftover herbs fade away; make Creamy Chimichurri (page 145) or Green Goddess Dressing (page 139) to enliven any grilled meat, veggies, or greens.

CHICKEN-VEGGIE PAN FRY
with GLASS NOODLES

Serves 4 generously

Korean japchae was the inspiration for this dish, but I've supersized the veggie quotient and scaled back the noodles to make it even tastier and better for you. You get a bit of chicken, glass noodles, mushrooms, red bell pepper, bok choy, and snow peas in every bite, all blanketed with a bit of savory sauce. Leftovers make for an A+ school lunch, either warmed or at room temperature.

6 dried shiitake mushrooms

3 ounces glass noodles

⅓ pound (about 20) green beans, trimmed

2 tablespoons soy sauce

1 teaspoon toasted sesame oil

1 teaspoon sugar

4 teaspoons neutral oil, such as avocado or canola

1 pound chicken tenders or 2 small boneless, skinless chicken breasts, cut into thin strips

1 teaspoon kosher salt

1 red bell pepper, cored and cut into thin strips

½ medium onion, sliced

1 medium carrot, peeled and shredded

2 garlic cloves, minced

4 ounces snow peas

½ head bok choy, sliced crosswise ½ inch thick

¼ teaspoon ground black pepper

¼ cup roasted cashews, coarsely chopped

Place the shiitake mushrooms in a bowl with enough hot water to cover them, and set aside to soften for 10 or 15 minutes.

Bring a large pot of water to a boil. Add the noodles and green beans, return to a boil, and cook until the noodles are nearly cooked through, about 4 minutes. Drain the noodles and beans, rinse under cold water, and set aside. Drain and slice the shiitakes, discarding the stems and reserving the soaking liquid.

In a small bowl, stir together the soy sauce, sesame oil, sugar, and 2 tablespoons of the reserved mushroom soaking liquid. Set aside.

In a wok or a large skillet, heat 3 teaspoons of the oil over medium-high heat. Add the chicken, sprinkle with ½ teaspoon of the salt, and cook, stirring often, until lightly browned and cooked through, about 7 minutes. Transfer to a bowl and set aside.

Add the remaining 1 teaspoon of oil to the pan along with the bell pepper, onion, and carrot and stir-fry until they start to soften, about 3 minutes. Add the garlic, snow peas, bok choy, sliced shiitakes, and 2 tablespoons of their soaking liquid. Season with the remaining ½ teaspoon salt and the pepper. Continue cooking and tossing until the vegetables are wilted, another 3 or 4 minutes.

Return the chicken, noodles, and green beans to the pan and toss to mix with the vegetables. Stir in the soy sauce mixture and cook until everything is heated through. Add the cashews, toss once more, and serve.

Glass noodles are fabulous in Wellness Soup (page 123) or as a stand-in for rice vermicelli noodles in spring rolls (page 94).

EGGPLANT *and* TOFU STIR-FRY *with* THAI BASIL

Serves 2

Eggplant fried with a generous handful of Thai basil was a popular side at my parents' restaurant. I've added cubes of fried tofu to make it a hearty entrée. The Thai basil is what makes it really special; its mild licorice fragrance and spicy, herbal flavor really lift the whole dish. In my parents' version, the eggplant is flash-fried to preserve its bright purple color, but here I prefer to preserve my waistline, so I air-fry it and the tofu instead!

1 pound firm tofu

¼ cup chicken or vegetable broth

1½ tablespoons hoisin sauce

1 tablespoon black vinegar

½ tablespoon dark soy sauce

Ground black pepper

2 Japanese eggplants (about 12 ounces total)

Kosher salt

Avocado oil cooking spray

2 teaspoons cornstarch

2 tablespoons neutral oil, such as avocado or canola

½ onion, sliced

2 garlic cloves, minced

½ cup loosely packed Thai basil leaves

Cooked jasmine rice, for serving

Halve the tofu horizontally into two slabs and wrap them in a kitchen towel. Place a weight, such as a heavy book or a pot, on top while you prepare the remaining ingredients; this will press out some of the water from the tofu and make it firmer.

In a small bowl, stir together the chicken broth, hoisin sauce, vinegar, soy sauce, and ¼ teaspoon of pepper, and set aside.

Cut the eggplant lengthwise into approximately 1-inch strips, then cut each strip into 1-inch pieces, rolling the strips after each cut to form irregularly shaped chunks. Place them in a large bowl, spray them lightly with the avocado oil cooking spray, and season with salt and pepper. Place the eggplant in the basket of your air fryer, spray lightly with oil, and air-fry at 380°F for 5 minutes, tossing once halfway through. (Depending on the size of your air fryer, you may need to do this in two batches.) Transfer the fried eggplant to a plate.

Slice the pressed tofu into 1-inch cubes and place them in the same bowl you used for the eggplant. Sprinkle with cornstarch and toss to coat the tofu evenly. Spray the tofu lightly with oil and toss again. Air-fry at 380°F for 8 minutes, tossing once halfway through, or until the tofu has lightly browned and is a bit crisp.

While the tofu cooks, heat the oil in a wok or a large skillet over medium-high heat. When the oil shimmers, add the onion and stir-fry for 2 minutes, then add the garlic and cook for another minute. Add the eggplant and sauce mixture and toss to coat; stir-fry for 2 minutes. Add the tofu and basil and continue to cook, stirring constantly, until everything is well combined and heated through. Serve hot over rice.

❋ *Black vinegar is also an essential ingredient in The Very Best Dumpling Sauce (page 41).*

VIETNAMESE SHRIMP *and* EGG OMELET

Serves 4

When my brothers and I were kids, money was often tight, and my parents had to be smart about making our limited food budget go as far as possible, especially when it came to proteins like meat and seafood. This savory omelet was frequently on the dinner menu; it's nothin' fancy, but with rice, it's a simple and satisfying dinner that stretches a handful of shrimp to feed four. As the name suggests, this is also a lovely breakfast or brunch dish. Serve it with sliced avocado and some Chili Garlic Oil (page 38) for drizzling.

6 large eggs

1 plum tomato

8 large shrimp, peeled and deveined

¼ cup sliced scallions (white and green parts)

1½ teaspoons fish sauce

½ teaspoon sugar

¼ teaspoon ground black pepper

4 teaspoons neutral oil, such as avocado or canola

Hot cooked jasmine rice, for serving

In a medium bowl, whisk the eggs until they're broken up and homogenous. Halve the tomato lengthwise and squeeze it gently, cut-side down, to remove the seeds and liquid. Dice the tomato into ½-inch pieces and add it to the bowl. Cut the shrimp into ½-inch pieces and add it to the egg mixture along with the scallions, fish sauce, sugar, and pepper. Whisk well to combine.

Heat the oil in a 12-inch nonstick skillet over medium-high heat. Add the egg mixture, reduce the heat to low, and cover with a lid. Cook for 12 minutes, then lift an edge of the omelet to check the bottom. If it is not nicely browned, cover the pan again and cook for another few minutes until the top of the omelet is set and the bottom is brown and crisp. Cut into quarters and serve with the rice.

✻ *Frozen shrimp is a great resource to have on hand, as you can use just what you need. If you defrosted more than you needed or want to use up a bag, my Shrimp Sushi Bake (page 151), Skinny Spring Rolls (page 94), or Vermicelli Bowls with Grilled Shrimp and Pickled Veggies (page 132) are just a few of the ways they can be put to good use!*

SAUCY SESAME SALMON, TWO WAYS

Serves 4

We eat salmon frequently in my house, but it never feels same-same because there are just so many different ways to prepare it. Of course, much depends on the sauce, so here I am giving you a choice of two that complement a quickly pan-seared, crusted fillet: a creamy (and lightened-up) version of bang bang sauce, and a bright, tart citrus sauce. I know many people have reservations about cooking fish with the skin on, but when it is cooked slowly in a cold pan as it is here, all the fat renders out of the skin, making it crispy and delicious, and it also protects the fish from overcooking. I think using black and white sesame seeds looks prettiest, but it will taste equally good with just one or the other.

1½ pounds salmon fillets, cut into 4 (5-ounce) portions (see My Tip)

2 teaspoons My Spice Blend (page 29)

2 tablespoons white sesame seeds

2 tablespoons black sesame seeds (or an additional 2 tablespoons white sesame seeds)

BANG BANG SAUCE

½ cup plain Greek yogurt

½ cup sweet chili sauce

½ cup sriracha

SOY-CITRUS SAUCE

¼ cup soy sauce

3 tablespoons fresh lemon juice

1 tablespoon fresh lime juice

2 teaspoons rice vinegar

1 teaspoon mirin

Arugula or shredded green cabbage, for serving

Sliced scallion greens, for garnish

Pat the salmon fillets dry and sprinkle both sides with the spice blend. In a shallow bowl, stir together the white and black sesame seeds. One at a time, dip the fillets, flesh-side down, into the seeds to create an even crust.

Arrange the salmon fillets, seeded-side up, in a nonstick skillet over medium-high heat. Cook the fillets without moving them until the skins loosen from the pan and turn golden brown and crisp, about 10 minutes. Carefully flip the fillets and cook seeded-side down for about 3 more minutes, or until the salmon is just cooked through.

While the salmon cooks, make one (or both) of the sauces. For the bang bang sauce, combine the Greek yogurt, chili sauce, and sriracha in a small bowl, and stir until well combined. To make the soy-citrus sauce, combine the soy sauce, lemon and lime juices, vinegar, and mirin in a small bowl, and stir until well combined.

Make a bed of arugula on four serving plates and top each one with a warm salmon fillet. Sprinkle with the scallions and serve with your choice of sauce.

My Tip: When you buy a large salmon fillet, you will want to do a bit of trimming to get picture-perfect fillets that cook evenly. Trim off the flat, thinner portion of the fillet and either freeze (if not previously frozen) or air-fry it for 6 or 7 minutes at 380°F, and use in Firecracker Salmon (page 100), the Shrimp Sushi Bake (page 151), or the Grilled Salmon Skewers on Tangy Noodle Salad (page 135).

❋ *Use any leftover soy-citrus sauce where you would reach for ponzu, including Broccoli with Bean Sprouts (page 202) or Clay Pot Chicken (page 173).*

FLASH-FRIED FLOUNDER *with* QUICK PINEAPPLE SALSA

Serves 4

Much as I love salmon, there are plenty of other fish in the sea, and now and then it's nice to change things up. If the people you cook for claim that white fish fillets, like flounder, fluke, or sole, are just too boring, this recipe may change their minds. These perfectly crisp fillets are topped with a lively pan-cooked salsa that is so much tastier than an old-school butter sauce (and a whole lot better for you!). Once you've got the salsa ingredients prepped, the whole dish comes together in about 10 minutes.

4 thin fish fillets, such as flounder or sole, about 6 ounces each (see My Tip)
2 teaspoons My Spice Blend (page 29)
2 tablespoons rice flour
1 tablespoon neutral oil, such as avocado or canola

QUICK PINEAPPLE SALSA
¼ cup chopped onion
1 large shallot, sliced
2 garlic cloves, minced
1 large plum tomato, diced
1 cup small-dice fresh pineapple
2 teaspoons fish sauce
1 teaspoon sugar
1 Thai chile, thinly sliced

Pat the fish fillets dry and sprinkle both sides with the spice blend. Dust liberally with the rice flour and shake off the excess.

Heat the oil in a large, nonstick skillet over medium-high heat. Add the fillets and cook until nicely browned on one side, about 3 minutes. Flip the fillets and cook until they are just cooked through and flake easily with a fork, another 2 to 4 minutes, depending on the thickness of your fish. Transfer to a plate.

To make the pineapple salsa: Reduce the heat to medium and add the onion, shallot, and garlic to the same skillet. Cook until they just begin to soften but not brown, 1 to 2 minutes. Add the tomato, pineapple, fish sauce, sugar, and chile, and cook until just heated through, another 2 minutes.

Spoon the salsa over the fish and serve immediately.

My Tip: Don't get hung up on using one particular variety of fish; often what's on sale has the highest turnover, so it's the freshest. This recipe will work with just about any kind of white fish fillets, including red snapper, cod, or even halibut; just increase the fish cooking time by an extra minute or two on each side to compensate for the extra thickness of the fillets, and be sure it flakes easily with a fork before you remove it from the pan.

✻ *Use the extra pineapple to make Tamarind Soup with Salmon, Tomatoes, and Pineapple (page 128).*

MAHI MAHI TOSTADAS
with FRUITY SLAW

Makes 8 tostadas, serves 4

If you like fish tacos, you will love these tostadas, which reverse the typical proportions of tortilla to fish. To keep things light yet flavorful, I've substituted a white bean mash for the more expected refried beans, and added pineapple and shredded snow peas to the eye-catching slaw for an explosion of sweet, salty, and fresh tastes in every bite!

3 (6-ounce) mahi mahi fillets
Kosher salt
1 tablespoon Kewpie mayonnaise
3 tablespoons Tajín seasoning

FRUITY SLAW
1 cup shredded red cabbage
1 carrot, shredded or julienned
½ cup (about 1 ounce) snow peas, finely julienned
1½-inch slice fresh or canned pineapple, thinly shredded
2 tablespoons chopped fresh cilantro
¾ teaspoon kosher salt
Juice of 1 lime

BEANS
1 (15-ounce) can Great Northern or navy beans, rinsed and drained
2 tablespoons chicken broth
½ teaspoon ground cumin
½ teaspoon salt

8 tostada shells
Lime wedges, for serving

Preheat your air fryer to 375°F.

Pat the mahi mahi fillets dry and season with salt. Spread one side of each fillet with 1 teaspoon of Kewpie mayo, then dust generously with the Tajín. Air-fry the fillets for 10 minutes. If the fish does not flake easily, air-fry for another 2 minutes. Transfer to a plate and set aside.

While the fish cooks, make the slaw. In a large bowl, combine the cabbage, carrot, snow peas, pineapple, cilantro, salt, and lime juice and toss well. Set aside.

To make the beans: In a medium microwave-safe bowl, combine the beans and chicken broth. Season with the cumin and salt and microwave on high until the liquid is bubbling, about 2 minutes. Use a potato masher or a wooden spoon to crush the beans into a rough puree.

To serve, spread each tostada shell with some of the mashed beans. Toss the slaw again (it will have released some moisture), and mound 2 tablespoons onto each tostada. Break the fish into chunks, arrange a few pieces atop each tostada, and serve warm with the lime wedges.

✳ *Tostada shells come in a package of twenty or more, so use the leftovers as you would tortilla chips or as a scoop for Broccoli Hummus (page 90) or Chili Beef Skillet Dinner (page 179).*

POOR MAN'S
CIOPPINO

page 166

POOR MAN'S CIOPPINO

Serves 6

Cioppino is the quicker, more straightforward cousin of French bouillabaisse and was traditionally made with whatever a fisherman had left over at the end of the day. Feel free to use any seafood you like, including crab or scallops, or do as I do and keep costs in check with affordable but flavorful mussels, shrimp, and the veggie doppelgängers for scallops—king oyster mushrooms. For the fish, I often grab frozen fillets, another budget-friendly move. I find many versions of cioppino too tomatoey—more like spaghetti sauce than a stew—so I add only 1 cup of canned tomatoes. Adjust to taste or add a few squirts of tomato paste if that's your preference.

3 tablespoons extra-virgin olive oil

2 king oyster mushrooms, cut into ½-inch slices

2 leeks, well-rinsed and thinly sliced

1 small fennel bulb, thinly sliced, some fronds reserved for garnish

1 medium carrot, peeled and sliced

2 lemongrass stalks, tough outer layers discarded, smashed (optional)

2 (½-inch-thick) slices fresh ginger

Kosher salt and ground black pepper

1 cup canned diced tomatoes with their juices

4 cups chicken broth, homemade (page 115) or store-bought

1 pound mussels, scrubbed

4 ounces squid, bodies cut into rings

8 ounces large shrimp, peeled and deveined

8 ounces firm white fish fillets, such as cod, cut into 2-inch pieces

1 tablespoon fish sauce

Toasted bread, for serving

Heat 2 tablespoons of the olive oil in a large, heavy pot over medium-high heat. Add the mushrooms in a single layer and cook without moving them for 2 minutes or so, until they are nicely browned. Flip them over and brown the other side for another 2 minutes, then transfer the mushrooms to a plate.

Add the remaining 1 tablespoon of oil to the pot along with the leeks, fennel, carrot, lemongrass (if using), and ginger. Reduce the heat to medium, season with salt and pepper, and sauté until the vegetables have softened, about 5 minutes. Add the tomatoes, mushrooms, and chicken broth. Bring to a simmer, cover, and cook for 15 minutes to blend the flavors. Discard the lemongrass.

Add the mussels and squid to the pot, then arrange the shrimp and fish on top of them. Return to a simmer, then cover the pot and cook for 3 minutes. Uncover the pot and check to see if the mussels have opened; if not, cover the pot again and cook for another minute, discarding any that have not opened. Add the fish sauce to the pot and gently stir everything to combine. Taste and season with salt, pepper, or more fish sauce if desired.

To serve, divide the cioppino among six shallow bowls. Garnish with the reserved fennel fronds and serve with toasted bread for dipping.

✳ *Extra king oyster mushrooms make great french fries; check out Air-Fryer Steak with Mushroom "Frites" on page 180.*

SHEET-PAN FIVE-SPICE CHICKEN LEGS *with* SQUASH *and* BROCCOLINI

Serves 4 to 6

Before there was pumpkin-spice seasoning (I mean looong before!), there was Chinese five-spice powder, a super-fragrant blend of cinnamon, cloves, and star anise with white pepper and fennel seed that fills your house with the most amazing aromas as it cooks. Here, I've mixed it with a squirt of sriracha and a pinch of brown sugar for an easy sheet-pan meal with lots of flavor. Blanching the Broccolini is an extra step, but it makes for a far more tender final result, so I think it's worth the minimal effort.

2 bunches Broccolini, bottom inch of the stems trimmed

4 teaspoons sriracha

1 tablespoon soy sauce

1 tablespoon brown sugar

2 large garlic cloves, grated or pressed

2 teaspoons peeled, grated fresh ginger

2 teaspoons Chinese five-spice powder

4 chicken legs and/or thighs, about 2½ pounds total

3 teaspoons kosher salt

1¾ teaspoons ground black pepper

3 tablespoons neutral oil, such as avocado or canola

1 small delicata squash, halved, seeded, and cut into half-moons

2 red onions, cut into thin wedges

8 ounces baby Yukon Gold potatoes or other small potatoes, halved

½ bunch cilantro, chopped

Bring a large pot of salted water to a boil. Add the Broccolini and cook for 3 minutes, then drain well and set aside.

In a large bowl, combine the sriracha, soy sauce, brown sugar, garlic, ginger, and five-spice powder and mix well. Season the chicken all over with 1 teaspoon of the salt and ¾ teaspoon of the pepper, then rub with 2 tablespoons of the sriracha-spice mixture.

Add the oil, the remaining 2 teaspoons of salt, and the remaining 1 teaspoon of pepper to the bowl with the sriracha-spice mixture and mix well.

Preheat the oven to 425°F. Place a rimmed baking sheet in the oven to preheat.

Add the blanched Broccolini, squash, onions, and potatoes to the bowl with the oil and spices and toss well to coat. Carefully remove the preheated baking sheet from the oven and arrange the vegetables on the pan in a single layer. Nestle the chicken pieces among the veggies and drizzle with any remaining spice-oil mixture from the bowl.

Roast until the chicken skin is brown and crisp and the potatoes are tender, about 30 minutes. Sprinkle with the cilantro and serve hot.

✿ *Five-spice powder adds a ton of flavor to almost everything. It's in my handy spice blend (page 29), it seasons the tofu in my Buddha Bowl (page 131), and I add it to Thanksgiving Baked Oat Muffins (page 65), too!*

SHEET-PAN FIVE-SPICE
CHICKEN LEGS *with*
SQUASH *and* BROCCOLINI

page 167

GRILLED LEMONGRASS CHICKEN THIGHS

Serves at least 4

We eat mostly dark-meat chicken at my house because it just has so much more flavor and is much less prone to drying out during cooking than chicken breasts. Here, a simple, garlicky, lemongrass-scented marinade and a bit of char from the grill (or a grill pan) give skin-on, boneless thighs a ton of flavor. If you can buy boneless thighs with the skin on, great; if not, it is really a snap to bone them yourself. If you just can't deal with that, boneless, skinless thighs are the next best thing. This makes a generous quantity because I *know* you'll want leftovers.

8 skin-on, boneless chicken thighs or whole thighs

1½ tablespoons My Spice Blend (page 29)

⅓ cup Lemongrass Shallot Paste (page 30)

2 tablespoons neutral oil, such as avocado or canola

2 teaspoons fish sauce

Cooked rice or vermicelli noodles, for serving

2 red Thai chiles, thinly sliced

2 scallions, green parts only, thinly sliced

Nuoc Cham (page 39), for serving

If your chicken thighs have bones, use a sharp knife to quickly and easily free the bone as follows: Place each thigh on a cutting board, skin-side down, and scrape along either side of the bone with the tip of the knife until the bone is exposed from end to end. Slip the point of the knife underneath the bone and gently work it toward either end until the bone comes free from the meat. Repeat with the remaining thighs. Trim off any excess bits of fat or flaps of skin. Sprinkle the thighs on both sides with the spice blend.

In a large bowl, combine the lemongrass paste, oil, and fish sauce. Add the chicken and massage the mixture into the chicken. Marinate the chicken for 30 minutes at room temperature or up to overnight in the refrigerator, covered.

Heat a barbecue grill or a ridged grill pan over medium-high heat until it becomes quite hot. Add the chicken (you may have to work in two batches if you're using a grill pan) and cook skin-side down until the skin becomes crisp and slightly charred, about 3 minutes. Turn the chicken over, reduce the heat to medium (or move it to a cooler part of the grill), and continue grilling until it is cooked through, another 5 minutes or so. Transfer to a plate, cover loosely with foil, and let rest for 5 minutes.

Slice each thigh and arrange atop a serving of rice or noodles with the chiles and scallions. Serve hot with the nuoc cham.

✺ *You'll find a million ways to use the leftover chicken, starting with Banh "My" (page 108), as the protein in spring rolls (page 94), or in any of the chicken salads in Chapter 4.*

CLAY POT CHICKEN
(Clay Pot Optional)
Serves 4

Another deep cut from the family restaurant archives, Clay Pot Chicken was always one of our most popular menu items. Its familiar ingredients were unintimidating to diners uncertain about what to order at a Vietnamese spot, but it was also a deeply comforting dish, with an irresistible layer of crunchy rice. The directions below are for making this in a Dutch oven, but if you are inspired to invest in a few inexpensive clay pots, know that it makes for a very fun and special presentation—a fact I was reminded of when my brother recently unearthed a cache of the restaurant's original pots that had been in his garage for sixteen years. That inspired me to resurrect this recipe, and let's just say that my daughters scraped their pots clean!

6 ounces green beans, trimmed

4 tablespoons neutral oil, such as avocado or canola

2 garlic cloves, finely minced

4 boneless, skinless chicken thighs, cut into 1-inch pieces

½ cup baby king oyster mushrooms or canned straw mushrooms

2 tablespoons dark soy sauce

½ teaspoon kosher salt

¼ teaspoon ground black pepper

¼ cup ponzu

2 tablespoons oyster sauce

1 teaspoon brown sugar

3 cups cooked jasmine rice

In a large pot of salted water, cook the green beans just until crisp, about 3 minutes. Drain the beans, cut them into 2-inch pieces, and set aside.

In a large skillet over medium-high heat, heat 2 tablespoons of the oil and the garlic. When the garlic starts to sizzle, add the chicken pieces and mushrooms, drizzle with the dark soy sauce, and sprinkle with salt and pepper. Cook, stirring, until the chicken is lightly browned on all sides, about 6 minutes. Add the ponzu, oyster sauce, and sugar and simmer until the chicken is cooked through, another 4 or 5 minutes. Stir in the green beans and remove from the heat.

Brush the bottom of a medium Dutch oven or a large, heavy-bottomed saucepan with the remaining 2 tablespoons of oil. Add the rice, pressing it firmly onto the entire bottom of the pan. Spoon the chicken mixture on top of the rice, spreading it evenly, and drizzle the pan juices evenly over everything. Place the pan over medium-high heat, cover, and cook until you can hear the rice beginning to pop and sizzle, about 8 minutes.

Serve immediately, making sure to scoop up some of the crispy rice with each spoonful.

✳ *Finish off the oyster sauce by making a Warm Shaking Beef Salad (page 184) or Sautéed Chinese Broccoli with Oyster Sauce (page 198).*

MOM *and* DAD'S TURMERIC CHICKEN *and* RICE BAKE

Serves 4

Chicken and rice recipes exist in just about every culture, and without exception, they are economical, homey, filling dishes that satisfy a range of palates. This is pure Vietnamese comfort food that can be assembled in minutes and on the table in well under an hour. My parents would have served this just as is, but I've added peas, mushrooms, and okra to the pan to make this a true one-dish wonder.

4 large chicken thighs

1½ teaspoons My Spice Blend (page 29)

1 tablespoon neutral oil, such as avocado or canola

1 small carrot, diced

1 large celery stalk, diced

½ small onion, diced

1 cup sliced cremini or king oyster mushrooms

1 tablespoon minced garlic

1 teaspoon kosher salt

2 tablespoons ground turmeric

¾ cup raw jasmine rice, rinsed and drained

1½ cups chicken broth, homemade (page 115) or store-bought

1 cup frozen green peas (no need to thaw)

½ cup sliced young okra (optional; see My Tip)

1 tablespoon unsalted butter

1 tablespoon fresh lemon juice

Preheat the oven to 350°F.

Pat the chicken dry and sprinkle both sides with the spice blend. Heat the oil in a Dutch oven or a large, ovenproof skillet over medium heat. Add the chicken and cook skin-side down without moving until the skin has rendered its fat and is deep golden brown, about 8 minutes. Transfer the chicken to a plate.

Add the carrot, celery, onion, and mushrooms to the pan, and sauté them in the rendered chicken fat until they start to soften, about 4 minutes. Add the garlic, salt, and turmeric and sauté until the garlic is fragrant, about 1 minute. Add the rice to the pan and stir to coat it in the seasonings. Add the chicken broth and bring to a simmer over medium-high heat. Nestle the chicken into the rice, skin-side up, and bake uncovered for 15 minutes. Stir the peas, okra (if using), and butter into the rice, and return the pan to the oven for another 3 minutes, or until the rice is tender.

Sprinkle with the lemon juice and serve immediately.

My Tip: Don't knock okra 'til you've tried it! The slimy texture that many people object to develops only when the pods are cooked for a long time; cooked crisp-tender, as they are here, they have an appealing texture similar to asparagus. Don't use large, mature okra pods, though, as they will be too tough and woody. If you have extra raw okra, add it to the salmon and tamarind soup on page 128.

GLAZED TURKEY MEATBALLS *on* SPAGHETTI SQUASH

Serves 4 to 6

There's no question that turkey meatballs are a healthier option than those made with beef or pork, but let's be real, they can be a bit bland or dry. Mine are loaded up with cottage cheese for extra protein and grated zucchini to keep them moist, then coated with a zingy glaze. This makes plenty of meatballs, so go ahead and freeze some for another meal if you like.

1 medium spaghetti squash, about 1 pound

1 small zucchini, grated

2 teaspoons kosher salt

½ cup cottage cheese, excess liquid drained

2 eggs

1 package ground turkey, about 1⅓ pounds

3 scallions (white and green parts), finely chopped

6 tablespoons almond flour

¼ teaspoon Chinese five-spice powder

2 garlic cloves, grated or minced

½ teaspoon grated fresh ginger

½ teaspoon ground black pepper

½ cup Tamarind Ketchup (page 36)

½ cup chicken broth, homemade (page 115) or store-bought

Preheat the oven to 350°F. Line a large, rimmed baking sheet with parchment paper.

Halve the squash crosswise and use a large spoon to scoop out the seeds. Place the squash in a baking pan cut-side down and add about ½ inch of water to the pan. Roast until the squash can be pierced easily with a fork, about 40 minutes.

While the squash bakes, make the meatballs. Place the zucchini in a colander and sprinkle with ½ teaspoon of the salt. Toss and set aside to drain in the sink for 10 minutes, then gather the shreds into a ball and squeeze to release some of their moisture.

In a large bowl, mash the cottage cheese with a wooden spoon to break up any large curds. Add the eggs and use a fork to combine thoroughly. Add the zucchini, turkey, remaining 1½ teaspoons salt, scallions, flour, five-spice powder, garlic, ginger, and pepper. Mix well.

Form the mixture into balls about the size of golf balls and arrange them on the lined baking sheet. Place in the oven and bake until the meatballs turn golden in places, about 20 minutes. Remove the meatballs and squash from the oven and turn the oven to broil.

Place the tamarind ketchup in a large bowl, add the meatballs, and toss them to coat with the ketchup. Return the meatballs to the baking sheet and broil until they're slightly caramelized, shaking them once or twice to keep from sticking, about 3 minutes. Transfer to a plate. Use the chicken broth to deglaze the baking sheet, scraping up any browned bits.

Use a fork to shred the squash into long strands and mound it on a serving dish. Pour the pan juices over the squash, tossing to lightly coat the squash strands. Top with the meatballs and serve hot.

✻ *Bake a larger squash and use the extra shreds in place of pasta in the Chicken-Veggie Pan Fry with Glass Noodles on page 155, or substitute it for the slaw on the Mahi Mahi Tostadas (page 163).*

VIETNAMESE PORK TENDERLOIN

Serves 3 to 4

Many people say a Vietnamese restaurant can be judged by its grilled pork chops, which are typically made with very thinly cut chops and grilled until the sugar in the marinades is deeply caramelized. This pork tenderloin delivers the same flavors with less sugar, and you can make it right in the oven.

1 large pork tenderloin
(1 pound or more)

2 tablespoons Lemongrass
Shallot Paste (page 30)

1½ tablespoons fish sauce

1 tablespoon dark soy sauce

2 tablespoons brown sugar

1 tablespoon neutral oil, such
as avocado or canola

Use a sharp knife to remove any silver skin (the tough sinew that may cover part of the meat) from the pork tenderloin. In a medium bowl, combine the lemongrass shallot paste, fish sauce, soy sauce, and brown sugar to make a thick paste. Add the pork to the bowl and rub it all over with the paste. Cover with plastic wrap or a plate and refrigerate for at least 1 or 2 hours and up to overnight.

Preheat the oven to 425°F.

In an ovenproof skillet large enough to hold the pork tenderloin, heat the oil over medium-high heat. When the oil is hot, scrape off as much of the marinade from the pork as possible, reserving it, and carefully add the pork to the hot pan. Sear the pork on all sides until nicely browned, about 8 minutes total. Transfer the pork to a plate and add the reserved marinade to the skillet along with ¼ cup of water. Stir over medium-high heat, scraping up any brown bits from the bottom of the pan, then return the pork to the skillet.

Place the skillet in the oven and roast the pork for 10 minutes, turning it once or twice to coat it with the pan juices. Remove from the oven and allow it to rest for 10 minutes before slicing. Stir any juices that have accumulated around the meat into the pan juices and drizzle over the pork.

✻　*Pork tenderloins tend to come two to a package, so cook both and use any leftovers to make "Free" Pork and Mango Spring Rolls (page 94) or slice thinly and add to your favorite ramen or noodle soup.*

CHILI BEEF SKILLET DINNER

Serves 4 to 6

I think of this dish as a peacekeeper, the kind of thing I turn to when my kids are clamoring for a trip to Taco Bell and I don't want to blow my good intentions on something fried, fatty, and too cheesy. Other than the onion, this involves minimal prep and chopping, which is welcome when I've had a day. Cauliflower rice secretly bulks this up and keeps the lean beef mixture from getting too dry. For the fam, I spoon the chili mixture onto warm cheesy tortillas; for myself, I skip the cheese and scoop it up with tortilla chips. Either way, a healthy dollop of avocado sauce puts this over the top.

2 tablespoons neutral oil, such as avocado or canola

1 yellow onion, chopped

3 garlic cloves, chopped

1 tablespoon ground cumin

1½ teaspoons kosher salt

1 teaspoon smoked paprika

½ teaspoon ground black pepper

1 pound ground beef (I use 90 percent lean)

1 (15-ounce) can black beans, drained

1 (12-ounce) bag cauliflower rice

1 red serrano chile, thinly sliced (optional)

1 cup frozen or canned corn kernels

4 scallions (white and green parts), chopped

8 (6-inch) flour tortillas or tortilla chips

1½ cups grated Cheddar cheese

Avocado Sauce (page 42), for drizzling

Hot sauce, tomato salsa, or lime wedges, for serving

Preheat the oven to 300°F.

Heat the oil in a large skillet over medium heat. Add the onion and sauté until translucent, about 4 minutes, then add the garlic, cumin, salt, paprika, and pepper and stir until the garlic is fragrant, about 1 minute. Add the beef and cook until it starts to brown, breaking it up with a wooden spoon, about 8 minutes. The beef should be very highly seasoned at this point.

Add the black beans, cauliflower rice, red chile (if using), and corn and cook until everything is heated through and most of the liquid has evaporated, 3 to 4 minutes. Stir in the scallions and remove from the heat.

While the chili cooks, arrange the tortillas on a large baking sheet. Sprinkle evenly with the grated cheese and bake until the tortillas are warm and the cheese is melted, about 4 minutes.

Spoon the chili mixture onto the cheesy tortillas and drizzle with the avocado sauce. Roll up the tortillas and serve hot with your choice of condiments.

AIR-FRYER STEAK
with MUSHROOM "FRITES"

Serves 2

This may be the all-time best way to use an air fryer, and if you still haven't bought one, this could be the winning argument in favor of investing! The steak comes out perfect medium-rare every time and cleanup is a breeze. Pair it with some tangy homemade steak sauce and a tangle of shoestring mushroom "fries" and you have yourself a perfect date-night meal.

One 1-inch-thick New York strip steak, about 12 ounces

1 teaspoon My Spice Blend (page 29)

2 tablespoons mushroom bouillon powder

MUSHROOM FRITES

2 large king oyster mushrooms

1 tablespoon soy sauce

1 teaspoon toasted sesame oil

Kosher salt (optional)

MUSTARD STEAK SAUCE

¼ cup Tamarind Ketchup (page 36)

2 tablespoons Dijon mustard, smooth or grainy

Preheat the air fryer to 400°F for 10 minutes. While it heats, pat the steak dry on both sides and sprinkle all over with the spice blend and mushroom bouillon powder.

Air-fry the steak for 10 minutes for medium-rare doneness (if you're cooking more than one steak, you may need to increase the cooking time by 1 or 2 minutes), turning it once after 6 minutes. Place the steak on a plate to rest, tented loosely with aluminum foil, for 10 minutes.

While the steak cooks, make the mushroom frites. Use your fingers to shred the mushrooms lengthwise into long strips. Place the strips in a bowl, drizzle with the soy sauce and sesame oil, and toss to coat.

While the steak rests, air-fry the mushrooms at 380°F until they are cooked and crisp, about 12 minutes, tossing them once halfway through. Sprinkle with a little salt, if desired.

To make the mustard steak sauce: Stir the tamarind ketchup and mustard together in a small bowl.

Slice the steak and serve with the mushroom frites and the steak sauce on the side.

❋ *If your mushroom package contains more than you need, use the extras in Poor Man's Cioppino (page 166) or Mom and Dad's Turmeric Chicken and Rice Bake (page 174), or add them to a stir-fry.*

WARM SHAKING
BEEF SALAD

page 184

WARM SHAKING BEEF SALAD

Serves 4

Once in a while, my husband asks, "Do we have to have Vietnamese food all the time?" I always laugh, because to me it's not "Vietnamese food," it's just food! But he never complains when this rich, saucy beef dish is on the menu, even though it is one of *the* most iconic Vietnamese dishes you can name. True to form, I have made it into a more veggie-forward dish, letting the warm beef lightly wilt the greens. You can always serve it with just a bit of rice on the side for those who want it. Most recipes call for rib eye or beef tenderloin, but I find that a more gently priced sirloin works just as well.

1 tablespoon fish sauce

4 teaspoons soy sauce

2 teaspoons sugar

½ teaspoon ground black pepper

2 garlic cloves, minced

2 tablespoons oyster sauce

1 pound sirloin steak, cut into 1-inch cubes

2 bunches watercress, tough stems discarded

2 cups (about a half of a 5-ounce package) arugula

2 Persian cucumbers, halved lengthwise and sliced

2 cups grape tomatoes, halved

2 tablespoons neutral oil, such as avocado or canola

1 small onion, quartered and sliced into ½-inch-thick pieces

Juice of 1 lime

Hot cooked jasmine rice, for serving (optional)

In a medium bowl, combine the fish sauce, soy sauce, sugar, pepper, garlic, and oyster sauce. Add the beef cubes and toss to coat well. Set aside at room temperature for up to 30 minutes, or cover and refrigerate for up to 24 hours (but bring to room temperature before cooking).

In a large salad bowl, toss together the watercress, arugula, cucumbers, and tomatoes. Set aside until ready to serve.

Heat a large wok or a skillet over high heat. When the pan is nice and hot, add the oil and swirl to coat the pan. Add the onion and cook, tossing often, until it starts to turn a bit brown on the edges, about 2 minutes. Add the beef and marinade to the pan, spreading the meat in a single layer. Sear the beef without moving for 1 minute, then stir well and cook for another 30 seconds. Continue to cook, stirring every 30 seconds or so, until the meat is cooked on all sides, about 5 to 6 minutes total.

Scoop the beef, onion, and pan juices onto the salad. Deglaze the pan with the lime juice, scraping up all the meaty bits, and drizzle over the salad. Toss well to dress the veggies and wilt them slightly. Serve immediately, with rice on the side, if desired.

STEAK TACOS
with POBLANO CREMA

Makes 8 tacos, serves 4

This is a great way to give leftover steak a new life, but if you don't have any cooked steak on hand, a thin cut like skirt or hanger steak will cook up in the air fryer in literally minutes. Just dust it with a little chili powder and salt, cook at 400°F for about 7 minutes, turning once, and let it rest while you assemble the meal. The luscious "crema" is whipped up in the blender, and because it's based on cottage cheese, it's not only silky smooth, it also adds a bit of protein. Use whatever wrappers you like; there are many low-carb and even no-carb tortilla options these days, and a good old corn tortilla is naturally gluten-free.

POBLANO CREMA

4 tomatillos, husks removed

1 poblano pepper

1 jalapeño pepper

½ cup cottage cheese

1 scallion, cut in 3 pieces

½ teaspoon kosher salt

½ teaspoon grated garlic

Juice of ½ lime, or to taste

RADISH SALSA

4 radishes, halved and thinly sliced

½ white onion, cut into small dice

¼ cup chopped fresh cilantro

8 wrappers of choice, such as corn or flour tortillas, jicama wraps, or cheese wraps

8 ounces cooked steak, cut across the grain into strips

2 avocados, sliced

Lime wedges, for serving

To make the poblano crema: In an air fryer, roast the tomatillos and poblano and jalapeño peppers at 400°F until very tender, about 14 minutes. When they're cool enough to handle, discard the skins and remove the cores and seeds from the peppers.

Place the roasted veggies in a blender along with the cottage cheese, scallion, salt, and garlic. Blend until smooth and fluffy. Scrape down the sides of the blender, add the lime juice, and mix again. Combine the radish salsa ingredients in a small bowl.

Top each tortilla with several slices of steak and avocado, then drizzle generously with the poblano crema. Sprinkle with some radish salsa and serve with the lime wedges.

✳ *Use any extra poblano crema on eggs, fish, or a sandwich.*

Chapter 6

SIDES

*You Just Can't Have
Too Many Veggies!*

Salads on the Side

Fast and Fresh

From the Oven (or Air Fryer)

THERE ARE TWO WAYS TO THINK ABOUT SIDE DISHES: Maybe you just consider them supporting players for the meaty main event—and another box to tick off your to-do list. I prefer to look at them as an opportunity to add excitement, color, and texture to my plate that also gives me handy building blocks for jump-starting healthy, balanced meals later on. They feel much less like afterthoughts, the seat-fillers of the meal lineup, when viewed through that lens.

We all love a good one-pot meal that comes complete with protein, starch, and veggies, and you'll find plenty of those in this book. But when straightforward roast chicken, pan-roasted salmon fillet, or a grilled steak are on the menu as they so often are, you're going to want to give them some company. That's when I turn to quick but nutritionally dense sides like these to keep the meal balanced, satisfying, and visually appealing.

Texture is nearly as important to me as flavor when I'm putting together a meal, and nearly all these recipes combine crisp, crunchy elements with bright, fresh flavors—there's not a soggy steamed broccoli spear in the bunch. You'll find new ways to prepare old friends like green beans, Brussels sprouts, and yes, broccoli, and you might even cozy up to some less-familiar greens like morning glory and gai lan to add variety to the rotation. What you won't find are a bunch of starchy sides because, unless I'm eating rice or noodles (as is often the case), I do try to minimize carbs, especially later in the day.

But who needs potatoes when you can have a rainbow of gorgeous veggies on your plate? In nearly every case, these sides can be made in double batches and saved to bolster lunches and dinners down the line. Most are good warm, cold, or at room temperature, and work with practically any kind of protein. With that kind of versatility, what's not to love?

SPICY CUCUMBER SALAD

Serves 4

This salad is as much fun to make as it is to eat, with springy, spicy coils of crunchy cucumber in a highly seasoned dressing. The nifty helix effect is achieved by placing two chopsticks alongside the cucumbers before cutting them to prevent the knife from going all the way through; however, if you are intimidated by the fancy knifework, it will taste just as good with the cucumbers sliced into chunky rounds. Either way, be sure to salt the cukes well to release some of their moisture.

6 Persian cucumbers
2 tablespoons kosher salt
2 tablespoons rice vinegar
1 tablespoon minced garlic
1 tablespoon gochugaru (Korean red pepper powder)
1 tablespoon brown sugar
1 tablespoon soy sauce
1 tablespoon toasted sesame oil
2 tablespoons sesame seeds

Place a cucumber on your cutting board with a chopstick on either side. Using the chopsticks as a guide to prevent you from cutting all the way through the cuke, slice the cucumber at a 45-degree angle every ¼-inch. Now flip the cuke, and again, using the chopsticks to control the depth of your cuts, slice the cuke perpendicular to the chopsticks. You should now have a springy coil of cucumber. Repeat with the remaining cucumbers and place them in a colander. Toss with the salt and set them in the sink to drain for 15 minutes. Rinse the salted cukes and drain well.

Transfer the cucumbers to a mixing bowl. Combine the dressing ingredients in a small bowl and pour over the cucumbers. Toss to coat. The salad is crispest when eaten the day it is made, but it can be refrigerated for up to 3 days.

FURIKAKE POTATO SALAD

Serves 4 to 6

Up your picnic game with this pretty, furikake-flecked take on an American classic. The cauliflower not only makes it a much lighter dish (and obviously minimizes the carbs) it also makes it taste much fresher.

1½ pounds Yukon Gold potatoes, peeled and cut into ¾-inch chunks

½ head (about 1 pound) cauliflower florets

½ cup Kewpie mayonnaise

2 tablespoons furikake, homemade (page 32) or store-bought

Zest of 1 lemon plus 4 teaspoons lemon juice

2 teaspoons kosher salt

1 teaspoon sugar

1 small celery stalk with leaves, stalk thinly sliced

2 scallions (green parts only), thinly sliced

Bring a large pot of heavily salted water to a boil. Add the potatoes, return to a boil, and cook for 4 minutes. Add the cauliflower, return to a boil, and cook until the potatoes and cauliflower are just tender, about another 5 minutes. Drain well in a colander.

In a mixing bowl, combine the mayo, furikake, lemon zest and juice, salt, and sugar. Mix well. Add the celery stalk and leaves, potatoes, and cauliflower, and toss with the dressing. Top with the scallion greens.

❋ *The remaining raw cauliflower can be chopped fine in the food processor and used in the Chili Beef Skillet Dinner (page 179), or roasted along with the mushrooms on page 207.*

QUICK *and* TASTY BABY BOK CHOY

Serves 4

Baby bok choy is available just about everywhere these days, and it's a nice change from the ordinary, especially in winter months when not many fresh green vegetables can be found in the market. Charring the bok choy before giving it a quick stir-fry brings out its flavor while keeping that nice, crisp snap. This dish comes together so fast, too! Just be sure to rinse the bok choy well, as dirt often lurks around the root ends.

2 tablespoons chicken or vegetable broth

2 teaspoons soy sauce

2 garlic cloves, minced

½ teaspoon grated fresh ginger

8 heads baby bok choy, halved lengthwise, rinsed, and patted dry

2 tablespoons hoisin sauce

In a small bowl, stir together the chicken broth, soy sauce, garlic, and ginger. Set aside.

Heat a large skillet over medium-high heat until very hot but not smoking. Add the bok choy, cut-side down, and cook without moving it until the undersides are a bit charred, about 2 minutes. Turn the bok choy charred-side up, add the broth mixture, and cover the pan. Cook for 2 to 3 minutes, then uncover the pan, turn the heat to high, and cook, tossing gently, until the liquid is reduced and the bok choy is tender, about 1 minute. Drizzle with the hoisin sauce, toss again, and serve warm.

✳ *You can often buy big bags of baby bok choy at Asian markets at very reasonable prices. Use it in soups like Wonton Soup with Bok Choy on page 127 or stir-fries like the Chicken-Veggie Pan Fry on page 155. It can also be cooked like the Sautéed Tender Greens with Garlic on page 203 or the Sautéed Chinese Broccoli with Oyster Sauce on page 198.*

SAUTÉED CHINESE
BROCCOLI *with*
OYSTER SAUCE

page 198

SAUTÉED CHINESE BROCCOLI *with* OYSTER SAUCE

Serves 2 to 3

For reasons I will never understand, bok choy is about the only Asian vegetable that routinely shows up in most mainstream supermarket produce sections. As much as I enjoy bok choy, it is really just the tip of the iceberg when it comes to Asian greens. I especially like the whole family of flowering greens in the broccoli family, which are great in soups as well as simple stir-fries like this one. Their stems are completely edible and, unlike their Western counterparts, don't need peeling. You may find them labeled as *gai lan, choi sum,* or *Chinese broccoli,* and any of them will work here.

1 tablespoon neutral oil, such as avocado or canola

3 garlic cloves, thinly sliced

½ tablespoon minced fresh ginger

8 ounces gai lan, ends trimmed

8 ounces sugar snap peas (see the ✳ tip)

1½ tablespoons oyster sauce

Sesame oil and sesame seeds, for garnish

Combine the oil, garlic, and ginger in a wok or a large skillet and place over medium-high heat. Cook, stirring often, until the garlic is fragrant, about 2 minutes; don't let it brown.

Rinse the gai lan under cold water and add it directly to the pan with the water still clinging to its leaves. Raise the heat to high and stir-fry until its leaves start to wilt, 2 or 3 minutes. Add the sugar snap peas, toss to combine, and cover the pan. Steam for 3 minutes. Uncover the pan, drizzle with the oyster sauce, and toss to coat everything lightly with the sauce. Continue to cook, uncovered, until the gai lan stalks are crisp-tender, another 1 to 2 minutes.

Transfer to a serving platter, drizzle with a bit of sesame oil, and sprinkle with the sesame seeds. Serve hot.

✳ *Sugar snap peas are great cooked or raw, sliced into salads like the Green Goddess Chicken Chopped Salad (page 139), or used as dippers for your favorite hummus. Or make the Orzotto with Shrimp and Asparagus on page 152.*

WARM BRUSSELS SPROUTS *with* MUSTARDY DRESSING

Serves 4 to 6

Salads of raw shaved Brussels sprouts had a moment, but I like the sprouts better when they get a quick hit of heat. It blunts their cabbage-y bite, making them a perfect companion for all sorts of cool-weather meals. A quick spin in the microwave is all it takes to soften the leaves without dimming their pretty green color, and because I zap them right in their serving dish, there are no skillets to wash up. Opt for large Brussels sprouts if you have a choice—you'll get more leaves off of each sprout.

1 pound Brussels sprouts

1 small shallot, minced

1½ tablespoons apple cider vinegar

1 heaping teaspoon Dijon mustard (the grainy type is nice if you have it)

1 teaspoon honey

1 small garlic clove, grated or pressed

2 tablespoons olive oil

Kosher salt and ground black pepper

¼ cup shaved Parmesan cheese (optional)

Slice off the stem ends of the Brussels sprouts and peel off the individual leaves, adding them to a large bowl as you go; you should have about 5 cups (see the ❋ tip).

In a medium, microwave-safe bowl, whisk together the shallot, vinegar, mustard, honey, and garlic. Whisk in the olive oil in a slow stream until everything is thick and well combined. Season generously with salt and pepper. Add the sprout leaves and toss thoroughly to coat them with the dressing.

Microwave the sprouts on high for 1 minute, stir, then microwave again until the leaves are just tender but still bright green, about another 90 seconds. Sprinkle with the Parmesan (if using), toss one last time, and serve warm.

❋ *Save the cores of the Brussels sprouts for another dish, as it is hard to peel off those tight inner leaves. You can roast them on a sheet pan with onions and carrots, or use the slicing blade of your food processor to shred them for a slaw or sauté, or toss them into the skillet when you are pan-roasting some chicken thighs.*

WARM BRUSSELS
SPROUTS *with*
MUSTARDY DRESSING

page 199

BROCCOLI
with BEAN SPROUTS

Serves 4

This is good warm, chilled, or at room temperature and goes with just about any kind of meal. If you have cooked broccoli in the fridge—and you know I recommend that you do!—this is ready in mere minutes. Just combine the cooked broccoli and bean sprouts in a heatproof bowl and top with boiling water to reheat the broccoli and soften the sprouts. I like to use the top portion of the stems as well as the florets, slicing them thinly into star-like shapes.

1 large head or 2 small heads broccoli (about 1 pound)

8 ounces bean sprouts

¼ cup Soy-Citrus Sauce (page 158) or ponzu

Bring a large pot of salted water to a boil. While the water heats, cut off all but 2 inches of the broccoli stems and reserve them for another use. Peel the remaining stems, then slice the broccoli crosswise all the way up to the florets. Break the florets into small pieces.

Cook the broccoli florets and sliced stems for 3 minutes, then add the bean sprouts to the pot. Cook 1 minute longer, then transfer the veggies to a colander and drain well.

Transfer the vegetables to a serving bowl and drizzle with the soy-citrus sauce. Serve warm, or refrigerate and serve chilled or at room temperature.

✳ *Use the reserved broccoli stems in place of celery in any tuna or chicken salad, or cut it in chunks and cook along with the cauliflower in my Furikake Potato Salad (page 192).*

In Praise of Broccoli

If you have kids, you've probably steamed enough broccoli to last a lifetime, as it sometimes seems like it's the only veg they will eat! But when it comes to versatility, it's hard to beat broccoli. What other vegetable can be eaten cooked or raw, roasted, grilled, or mashed, and yields two different textures, from the tender florets to the crunchy stalks? Cooked broccoli also holds up well in the fridge, ready to toss into a bowl of pho or a stir-fry, mash into a tuna salad (really—check out page 109!), or add to any kind of vegetable salad. If you have declared a moratorium on broccoli, see if one of the recipes in this section won't persuade you to bring it back into the rotation.

SAUTÉED TENDER GREENS
with GARLIC

Serves 4

Use this recipe with any delicate, tender greens you like for a simple but refreshing side. My go-to is water spinach, those long, leafy stalks that are also known as morning glory, but the same method works well with pea leaves or even regular spinach. You get two different bites in every mouthful, as the thicker stems retain a bit of crunch while the leaves cook down to a silky softness.

1 tablespoon neutral oil, such as avocado or canola

4 garlic cloves, thinly sliced

1½ pounds tender greens, cut into 2- or 3-inch pieces

1 teaspoon fish sauce

½ teaspoon sugar

In a large skillet over medium heat, add the oil and garlic. Cook, stirring occasionally, until the garlic starts turning golden around the edges, 2 or 3 minutes.

Add the greens to the pan and use tongs to toss and coat them with the oil until they have wilted. Add the fish sauce and sugar and continue to toss until the leaves are tender but not mushy and the stems retain a bit of snap, 2 or 3 minutes, depending on which vegetable you are using. Serve immediately.

Wilted greens like these are the perfect addition to the Buddha Bowl (page 131) or a bowl of Steamed Eggs 101 (page 56).

WARM ROASTED BEET SALAD *with* CITRUS *and* FRIED SHALLOTS

page 206

WARM ROASTED BEET SALAD *with* CITRUS *and* FRIED SHALLOTS

Serves 4

Crunchy, salty, sweet, and tart—what more do you want in a winter side? It will taste just as good the next day, but the colors and textures are best if the salad is assembled right before serving, as the beets will stain the other ingredients. If you have more exotic citrus fruits to use up, like blood oranges or pomelos, go for it, but don't skip the fried shallots and dill—they really bring the diverse flavors together.

2 medium beets, scrubbed
½ cup extra-virgin olive oil
2 tablespoons fresh lemon juice
2 tablespoons red wine vinegar
½ teaspoon kosher salt
¼ teaspoon ground black pepper
8 ounces green beans, trimmed
1 navel orange, peeled and cut into segments
1 small grapefruit, peeled and cut into segments
½ head fennel, cored and thinly sliced
½ cup crumbled feta cheese
¼ cup Fried Shallots (page 33)
¼ cup chopped fresh dill

Preheat the oven to 425°F. Wrap the beets in aluminum foil and roast until they're tender and very easy to pierce with the tip of a knife, about 50 minutes.

In a medium bowl, combine the olive oil, lemon juice, vinegar, salt, and pepper and whisk until emulsified. When the beets are cool enough to handle, peel them (their skins should slip right off) and cut into thin wedges. Add the beets to the dressing, toss well, and set aside.

Bring a saucepan of salted water to a boil. Add the green beans and cook until tender, about 5 minutes. Drain and cut into 1-inch pieces. In a large serving bowl, combine the green beans with the orange and grapefruit segments, fennel, and feta. Add the beets and their dressing and toss to combine. Right before serving, top with the fried shallots and dill, toss again, and serve.

Use up the fennel in Poor Man's Cioppino (page 166) or Green Goddess Chicken Chopped Salad (page 139). I also like to use the tops and any wilted layers in Very Good Vegetable Broth (page 114).

GARLIC ROASTED MUSHROOMS

Serves 4

Don't be intimidated by the large quantity of mushrooms called for here. Mushrooms are like spinach: What looks like a huge pile when they're raw really shrinks down as they cook, concentrating their earthy flavor in the process. I prefer to make this in the oven because then I don't have to hover over them, plus you get lots of delicious brown bits, especially if you can find shaggy maitake mushrooms at your market. If you like, throw some green beans onto the pan along with the 'shrooms for a more colorful side.

2 tablespoons (¼-stick) unsalted butter

2 tablespoons extra-virgin olive oil

2 pounds mixed fresh mushrooms, such as button, shiitakes, or maitakes

6 garlic cloves, peeled and thickly sliced

6 to 8 thyme sprigs

Kosher salt and ground black pepper

¼ cup finely chopped fresh parsley

Juice of ½ lemon, or more to taste

Preheat the oven to 425°F. Place the butter and olive oil on a rimmed baking sheet and place in the oven to preheat.

While the butter melts, trim the mushrooms and cut them into halves or quarters, depending on their size (if using shiitakes, discard the stems). If using maitakes, rip each mushroom into small, bite-size clumps.

Remove the sheet pan from the oven and arrange the mushrooms, garlic, and thyme sprigs on it. Use tongs or a metal spatula to toss the mushrooms until they're evenly coated with the butter and oil. Season with salt and pepper.

Roast until the mushrooms are tender and golden brown on the edges here and there, about 16 minutes, tossing once after 8 minutes. Sprinkle with the parsley and lemon juice, toss again, and transfer to a serving bowl, making sure to scrape up all the yummy pan juices.

✳ *Go big on this—the leftovers are terrific in omelets, rice bowls, and a thousand other things, although if you make a double batch, you should use two sheet pans to allow the mushrooms to brown properly.*

CHARRED BROCCOLI
with LEMONY TAHINI SAUCE

Serves 4 to 6

This sounds fancy, but it all cooks together in the air fryer (or on a sheet pan in the oven) and couldn't be simpler to assemble. I like the way the broccoli looks in big slabs, but if you prefer, you can chop it into bite-size pieces and toss it with the dressing for a more salad-like presentation. Either way, it's not your boring old steamed broccoli!

2 broccoli crowns, stems trimmed

1 red onion, cut in thin wedges

Neutral oil, such as avocado or canola, as needed

1 large head garlic

3 tablespoons tahini

Kosher salt and ground black pepper

2 tablespoons fresh lemon juice

¼ cup roasted sunflower seeds

Preheat the oven to 400°F. (You can also do this recipe in an air fryer if you have one with multiple racks or a large enough capacity.)

Stand the broccoli crowns on their heads and slice down through the stems to create three thick slabs from each. (Try as best you can to line your cuts up with the way the vegetable naturally branches at the top so you don't have a lot of little pieces rolling around.) Arrange the broccoli slabs and onion wedges on a baking sheet or the air-fryer racks and spray or brush lightly on both sides with the oil.

Slice off the top quarter of the garlic head to expose the cloves and nestle it among the broccoli. Drizzle with a bit more oil.

Roast the broccoli and garlic for 16 minutes, then flip the broccoli only and continue to roast until it has a few golden spots on each side and both it and the garlic are tender, another 6 to 8 minutes. Alternatively, air-fry at 375°F for about 20 minutes, turning the broccoli once halfway through.

In a small bowl, stir the tahini to loosen it and add the squeezed pulp from 6 of the roasted garlic cloves (or more if you like—I'm not the boss of you!). Mash the garlic to combine it with the tahini, season with salt and pepper, and stir well to combine. The tahini will stiffen up, but that's okay. Add the lemon juice a little at a time and keep stirring until the sauce is smooth and pourable; taste and add more lemon juice or salt if needed. If the sauce is too thick, add a teaspoon of water.

Pour the sauce over the warm broccoli and serve sprinkled with the sunflower seeds.

209

SWEET POTATOES *with* HOT HONEY PEANUT BUTTER TOPPING

Serves 4

I'm not even sure how I discovered this, but I really love the flavor of peanut butter with sweet potatoes. The honey—just a touch—highlights the sweetness of the roasted potatoes. This would make a great Thanksgiving side dish; just peel and cube the potatoes and toss them with the sauce before sending them under the broiler for a quick char. I find Red Garnet sweet potatoes bake up the fluffiest and least fibrous, but any orange-fleshed variety will work.

2 good-sized sweet potatoes

Neutral oil, such as avocado or canola

2 tablespoons (¼-stick) unsalted butter, softened

2 tablespoons smooth peanut butter

2 teaspoons hot honey or plain honey

Small pinch of kosher salt

1 teaspoon sesame seeds (black ones look prettier!)

Preheat the oven to 400°F.

Rub the sweet potatoes all over with the oil and prick each one with the tip of a knife in five or six places. Place the potatoes on a baking sheet and roast until soft (but not collapsing) when squeezed, 45 to 55 minutes. Remove from the oven and turn the oven to broil.

In a small bowl, mash together the butter, peanut butter, honey, and salt until smooth and well combined. Halve the baked sweet potatoes lengthwise and spread with the peanut butter mixture. Return the potato halves to the oven and broil until brown, 2 or 3 minutes.

Sprinkle the potatoes with the sesame seeds and serve hot.

If your crew isn't keen on eating sweet potatoes in their skins, scoop out the flesh, mash, and top with the honey peanut butter before broiling. Then use the scooped-out skins to make Banh "My" sammies (page 108). You could also throw an extra sweet potato in the oven and use it to make Thanksgiving Baked Oat Muffins (page 65).

Chapter 7

SWEET!

Desserts and Treats
to Feel Good About

OF ALL THE CHAPTERS IN THIS BOOK, I probably struggled with this one the most. After all, this is supposed to be a healthy cookbook; I wasn't even sure I should include dessert recipes at all! On top of that, we never had sweets in the house when I was a kid; our family meals usually ended with fresh fruit of some kind, and to this day, cutting up a beautiful plate of fruit is my mother's love language. So it's not like I had a stash of family cake, cookie, or brownie recipes up my sleeve.

But even though we never had packaged cookies or chocolate in the house, I can't say I don't have a sweet tooth—quite the opposite. I hoarded my Halloween candy, doling it out piece by piece to make it last for months, and when *that* was gone, I would improvise a dessert by slathering butter and sugar onto a slice of bread. Even as an adult, I still have that urge for something sweet at the end of a meal. So, I challenged myself to create desserts that are indulgent and celebratory without any added refined sugar or wheat. The answer, as always (in a Vietnamese home, anyway) turned out to be a generous amount of nature's candy—fruit—and maybe just a skosh of chocolate.

Of course, fruit does contain carbs, but because it comes hand in hand with plenty of good fiber, it is metabolized differently (and more slowly) than, say, a cupcake. Fruit also contains nutrients, which those cupcakes just don't. And we all know that good dark chocolate has proven health benefits like anti-inflammatory properties while being relatively low in sugar.

To my surprise, it was easy to come up with desserts that met my criteria yet are packed with flavor, avoid fake sweeteners, and are lower in sugar than you'd expect from a treat. Most are rich enough that you won't need (or want) to eat a ton to feel satisfied. You could even go so far as to say that these are actually good for you, with added ingredients like tofu, cottage cheese, and chia seeds for a protein and nutritional boost, as well as fun extras like goji berries and popped quinoa. You'll be happy to have these healthy add-ins on hand to level up your breakfast bowls, too!

FRESH "CHAR-FRUIT-ERIE" BOARD

Serves as many as you want!

Who says charcuterie boards are only for apps? I think this bountiful display makes the perfect last course. I have enhanced the trompe l'oeil effect by adding some sliced chocolate salami and cutting the melon to look like slabs of cheddar. It's guaranteed to make everyone smile twice—once when they get the joke, and again when they enjoy the goodies.

Chocolate Salami (page 241)

1 ripe cantaloupe

1 ripe mango, peeled and sliced

Apples or pears, cut into wedges

Fresh berries

Red and green grapes, cut into small clusters

Chocolate-covered coffee beans or dark-chocolate-covered almonds

Salted, roasted almonds

Digestive biscuits

Spiced Orange Caramel Sauce (page 218), for dipping

Start by arranging a few small bowls or ramekins on your large serving board for the dips. Place the chocolate salami on the board.

Cut a thick wedge from the cantaloupe. Cut off the rind and remove the seeds, then cut in half crosswise. Slice each half wedge crosswise and arrange on the board, fanning the slices slightly as you would a wedge of Cheddar cheese. Fan out the mango slices in the same way.

Fill in the remaining gaps on the board with the apples, berries, grapes, chocolate-covered coffee beans, almonds, and digestive biscuits. Just before serving, warm the caramel in the microwave for about 30 seconds or until liquid and pour into one of the ramekins.

SPICED ORANGE CARAMEL SAUCE

Makes about 1 cup

Because it is made with dates, not sugar, this is a pretty goof-proof sauce that lends itself to improvisation. You could add a cinnamon stick, a bit of chai flavoring, or even a pinch of hot pepper flakes to tailor this to your preferences. Make sure to choose soft, tender Medjool dates, or the caramel will not blend up smooth and unctuous. You can make this ahead and refrigerate, but rewarm it before serving.

1 cup pitted Medjool dates
   (about 5 ounces), chopped
1 cup coconut milk
1 star anise pod or
   ⅛ teaspoon Chinese
   five-spice powder
2 (3-inch) strips orange peel
1 teaspoon unsalted butter
¼ teaspoon kosher salt

In a small saucepan, combine the dates, coconut milk, star anise, and orange peel, and bring to a simmer over low heat. Cook at a gentle simmer for 2 minutes, then remove from the heat. Stir in the butter and salt, cover, and set aside for 15 minutes.

Discard the orange peel and star anise, and transfer the mixture to a food processor. Puree until smooth, scraping down the sides once or twice. Serve warm or at room temperature.

❋ *Drizzle any leftover caramel sauce onto your Tin Roof Parfait (page 227), or stir some sauce into Greek yogurt and top with mandarin orange segments.*

THE JACKFRUIT PROJECT

Serves 8 or more, depending on the size of your jackfruit

Jackfruit has gained popularity among vegan cooks, who discovered that the texture of canned young jackfruit is a dead ringer for shredded or pulled meat in tacos, barbecue sandwiches, and even crab cakes. Fresh mature jackfruit, though, is a different thing entirely, and it's often the crowning touch on a big family meal at my house. It has a unique texture and flavor similar to a mango. When ripe, the succulent flesh needs no embellishments at all, but liberating those tasty morsels can be a bit of a project, which is why this isn't so much a recipe as a how-to guide. So, pull on a pair of gloves, get out your sharpest chef's knife, and prepare to be wowed.

1 fresh ripe jackfruit (or a half or quarter fruit if your market sells them)

Neutral oil, such as avocado or canola

The jackfruit's spiky green rind and large, smooth seeds are inedible; what you're after is the dense flesh that cushions the seeds and looks something like oversized kernels of corn. To get to it, you must use your hands to pluck out and discard the seeds, revealing the tender bites of jackfruit. When cut, though, this flesh exudes a sticky, glue-like sap that is hard to wash off, so I highly recommend donning a pair of food-prep gloves before tackling your jackfruit!

Start by choosing a ripe jackfruit, one whose spiky outer rind has some yellow spots. If you have bought a whole fruit, you'll want to section it into more manageable portions; for that, you'll need a large, sharp knife. That sticky sap will bond to your knife blade like cement, so oil the blade generously to minimize the accumulation of residue before you cut into the fruit.

Starting in the center, cut the jackfruit in half through its equator and then again into quarters to produce eight wedges. Arrange the wedges on a large platter and set the platter at the center of the table. Hand out gloves all around and let everyone go to town on their own portion. The leftovers can be refrigerated for up to a few days.

Glove Love

Wearing gloves when attacking a jackfruit is highly recommended, but in my house, that's about the only time you'll see me using them. I'm often asked by followers why I don't wear gloves, a hairnet, or other sanitary safeguards in my cooking videos. The answer is simple: Like you, I am cooking for myself and my family, not restaurant patrons or other members of the public, so those types of precautions just aren't necessary. When I make meatballs, fold dumplings, mix salad ingredients, and so on, I like to be able to feel the textures of the ingredients, and disposable gloves just get in the way. As long as I start and end with clean hands, it's all good.

LOADED FRUIT NACHOS

Serves 4 to 6

This is every bit as much fun to eat as a big platter of spicy nachos! Be sure to cut the fruit into small, salsa-like bits and drain it well so it's easy to scoop up with the chips and doesn't make them too soggy. Complete the illusion with a drizzle of "crema" and as many toppings as you like.

1 sweet apple, such as Pink Lady, peeled and cored

1 pint strawberries, hulled

2 kiwis, peeled

2 red or black plums, halved and pitted

2 teaspoons raw sugar

1 teaspoon grated orange zest

1 (5-ounce) bag unflavored plantain chips

½ cup Cashew Crème (page 231) or well-drained Greek yogurt

½ cup coconut shavings, toasted

8 to 10 mint leaves, finely chopped

2 tablespoons cacao nibs (or grated dark chocolate)

Cut the apple into ¼-inch-thick slices. Stack the slices and cut into ¼-inch strips, then cut the strips crosswise into ¼-inch cubes. Repeat with the strawberries, kiwis, and plums to make a confetti-like fruit salsa. Place the fruit in a large bowl and sprinkle with the sugar and orange zest, toss well, and set aside to macerate for 15 minutes or so.

Shake the plantain chips onto a large plate or platter, allowing them to mound randomly. Use a slotted spoon to arrange the fruit salsa atop the chips, reserving the liquid in the bowl. Stir the cashew crème into the reserved fruit liquid, then drizzle over the fruit and chips. Sprinkle with the coconut, mint, and cacao nibs, and place in the center of the table so everyone can dig in!

✳ *Sprinkle leftover cacao nibs on your Blue-on-Blue Smoothie Bowl (page 50) or Bark Bites with Quinoa Crunchies (page 240).*

TAPIOCA CHIA PUDDING
with MANGO

Serves 4 to 6

I've given tapioca pudding a bit of a makeover, Vietnamese-style, turning this old-fashioned favorite into a fresh-tasting, multi-textured comfort dessert. Chia seeds make it extra creamy; lime zest and toasted coconut give it brightness and crunch. Note that you will need to make this pudding ahead of time to give the chia seeds a chance to absorb the coconut milk. The fruity topping and garnishes really make this look restaurant-worthy!

¼ cup fine tapioca pearls
2 tablespoons chia seeds
1 (13.5-ounce) can full-fat coconut milk, well shaken
½ teaspoon kosher salt
2 tablespoons maple syrup
¼ cup unsweetened shredded coconut or coconut shavings
1 mango
Zest of 1 lime

Place the tapioca and chia seeds in a medium saucepan. Add the coconut milk, 1 can of water, and the salt. Stir to combine (the chia seeds will float to the surface, so just stir them in as best you can) and bring to a simmer over medium heat.

Let the pudding cook at a gentle simmer, stirring occasionally, until the tapioca has swelled and softened and the pudding has thickened, about 15 minutes. Stir in the maple syrup. Transfer to a bowl, cover, and refrigerate until well chilled, at least 1 hour.

When you're ready to serve: In a dry skillet over medium heat, toast the coconut, tossing frequently, until it is nicely browned, about 4 minutes. Transfer to a plate to cool.

Peel the mango, then slice off the flesh in large slabs from both sides of the flat pit. Slice or cube the mango. Spoon the chilled pudding into bowls or dessert cups and arrange some of the mango on top of each portion. Sprinkle with the coconut and a pinch of lime zest and serve.

VIETNAMESE FRUIT COCKTAIL

Serves 4

Fruit cubes swimming in a bath of icy-cold coconut milk may sound odd if it's new to you, but this is actually a very common dessert in Vietnamese homes and one of the most refreshing treats I know. My updated version is made with fresh fruit instead of canned, but it is just as eye-catching. You can use any fruits you like (or need to use up), but aim for a mix of colors and textures. You'll want about 3 cups total. And if you want to add some canned glass jelly from the Asian market for an authentic touch, go for it!

1 (15-ounce) can reduced-fat coconut milk

½ cup heavy cream or half-and-half (or coconut yogurt for a vegan option)

2 tablespoons agave nectar

1 cup cubed honeydew melon

½ cup halved green grapes

½ cup raspberries

½ cup cubed mango, peach, or nectarine

½ cup pomegranate seeds

Ice cubes

Grated zest of 1 lime, for garnish

In a large bowl, add the coconut milk, cream, and agave nectar and whisk to combine. Add the melon, grapes, raspberries, mango, and pomegranate seeds and stir. Refrigerate, covered, until ready to serve, or up to 4 hours.

To serve, place a handful of ice cubes in each of four dessert bowls or glasses. Spoon the fruit mixture and coconut milk over the ice. Garnish with the lime zest.

❋ *Toss extra green grapes into The Glow-Up Green Smoothie (page 49), or add them to the Green Goddess Chicken Salad (page 139) if they don't disappear at snack time.*

TIN ROOF PARFAIT

Serves 4

When I've had a dinner that's a little light on protein, this easy-to-assemble dessert tips the scales back in the right direction. It's another great showcase for cottage cheese, the comeback kid of the keto crowd, but if you haven't made your peace with cottage cheese yet, by all means swap in yogurt (in which case you won't need to chill the mixture). I use regular raw peanuts, but for that authentic old-timey look, red-skinned cocktail peanuts are the way to go. If dairy doesn't agree with you, go with coconut alternatives for the yogurt and heavy cream, and just leave out the cream cheese. In fact, I might even prefer it that way!

16 ounces low-fat cottage cheese, drained

4 ounces low-fat cream cheese, at room temperature

2 pitted dates (preferably Medjool), soaked in warm water for 5 minutes and drained

1 teaspoon vanilla extract

CHOCOLATE GANACHE

1 (3.5-ounce) bittersweet chocolate bar, chopped

¼ cup heavy cream or coconut milk

¾ cup peanuts, raw or roasted, salted and coarsely chopped

Cacao nibs, for garnish (optional)

In a blender or food processor, combine the cottage cheese, cream cheese, dates, and vanilla and puree until smooth. Scrape into a bowl, cover, and refrigerate until firm, at least 4 hours and up to 3 days.

When you're ready to serve, make the ganache. In a microwave-safe glass measuring cup, combine the chopped chocolate and heavy cream. Microwave on high in 30-second increments, stirring after each interval, until the ganache is completely smooth and pourable, about 1 minute total.

Sprinkle some of the peanuts into each of four dessert glasses. Top the peanuts with about ¼ cup of the cottage-cheese mixture and drizzle some of the ganache over it. Make another layer of peanuts, cottage cheese, and ganache, and end with a final sprinkle of peanuts and a few cacao nibs, if using.

Variations

This dessert is infinitely riffable, and it can make use of any fruits, nuts, or flavorings you happen to have on hand. Blend the cottage cheese with peanut butter powder, cocoa, maple syrup, or honey; add a layer of berries or other fruit; substitute Spiced Orange Caramel Sauce (page 218) for the chocolate ganache; grate dark chocolate on top; or substitute chopped pistachios or pecans for the peanuts. You get the idea.

❋   *If you have extra ganache, dip strawberries into the chocolate, then into chopped peanuts or cacao nibs. Store in the refrigerator in a paper-towel-lined covered container until ready to serve, or up to a day or two.*

MAPLE GINGER TOFU

Serves 4

I had forgotten all about this simple, elegant dessert until I attended a very swanky wine dinner in Napa Valley. After six stunning courses of exquisite food and wine pairings, the servers presented each of us with a pristine bowl of house-made tofu topped with delicate ginger syrup. The taste and texture instantly transported me back to childhood, as this was a dessert my mother made occasionally when I begged her for something sweet. At the time, I only wanted some Oreos; now I appreciate its subtle flavor and slippery, silky texture and plan to have it in my dessert repertoire going forward!

1½-inch piece fresh ginger
2 tablespoons maple syrup
1 pound silken tofu

Using a large, sharp knife, peel the ginger and slice it as thinly as you can. Stack the slices and cut them into fine slivers.

In a small saucepan over medium-high heat, combine the ginger, maple syrup, and ½ cup of water. Bring to a boil, then reduce the heat to low and simmer gently for 10 minutes. Remove from the heat.

Carefully slice the tofu into four blocks and place one into each of four dessert bowls. Drizzle with some of the ginger-maple syrup, top with some of the candied ginger shreds, and serve.

✻ *The ginger syrup would be a delicious addition to any fruit parfait or pudding, drizzled on pancakes, and added to the Vietnamese Fruit Cocktail (page 224)—or an actual cocktail for that matter!*

ROASTED APPLES *with* OAT CRUMBLE

Serves 4

If you are craving apple pie but can't be bothered with rolling out pie crusts (guilty!), this fall-flavored dessert will scratch that itch without the need for a rolling pin. I like to make this in individual portions, sort of like a baked apple, but if you prefer, spread the apples in a small baking dish, top with the crumble mixture, and bake for a more traditional crisp-like dessert.

½ cup rolled oats

¼ cup chopped pecans or walnuts

¼ teaspoon ground cinnamon

¼ teaspoon kosher salt

2 tablespoons maple syrup

1 tablespoon neutral oil, such as avocado or canola

1 tablespoon unsalted butter, softened

¼ teaspoon kosher salt

2 Granny Smith apples

Whipped cream, Cashew Crème (page 231), or Greek yogurt, for serving (optional)

Preheat the oven to 350°F.

In a medium bowl, combine the oats, pecans, cinnamon, and salt. Drizzle with the maple syrup and the oil and stir to coat well. Spread the oat mixture on a small rimmed baking sheet and bake for 20 minutes, stirring once about halfway through. Transfer to a bowl and set aside.

In a separate small bowl, mash the butter, maple syrup, and salt together until smooth and well combined. Peel and halve the apples, using a spoon or a melon baller to remove the cores. Arrange the apple halves in a 9 × 9-inch baking pan and dot small bits of the butter mixture onto the cut surface of the apples. Top the apples with the oat crumble mixture and cover the pan with aluminum foil.

Bake until the apples are tender when pierced with the tip of a knife, about 30 minutes. Serve as is or with a dollop of whipped cream, cashew crème, or Greek yogurt, if desired.

✳ *Here's a sitch where I urge you to plan for leftovers; this oat crumble mixture is really just granola by another name, and you can use it to top your breakfast yogurt or chia pudding, layer into a parfait, or just eat by the handful. So go ahead and double or even quadruple the recipe, then spread it on a large rimmed baking sheet and bake for 20 minutes, tossing once about halfway through.*

CASHEW CRÈME

Makes about 1 cup

Plan to use this on a Tin Roof Parfait (page 227), or top Heart-y Strawberry Pancakes (page 66) for an extra-festive breakfast, or just spoon a dollop onto your cold-brew coffee.

1 cup raw cashews
1 cup boiling water
1 small date, pitted
½ teaspoon vanilla extract
Pinch of kosher salt

Place the cashews in a heatproof bowl or glass measuring cup and cover with the boiling water. Set aside to soak for at least 30 minutes.

Drain the soaked cashews, reserving the soaking liquid, and place them in a blender with the date, vanilla, and salt. Add ½ cup of the soaking liquid and blend until the mixture is smooth and creamy. This may take a few minutes; just keep blending until it is satiny-smooth. If the mixture is too thick to blend easily, add more of the soaking liquid a teaspoon or two at a time. The crème can be refrigerated in a covered container for up to 5 days.

GRILLED PINEAPPLE
with HOT HONEY *and*
QUESO FRESCO

page 234

GRILLED PINEAPPLE *with* HOT HONEY *and* QUESO FRESCO

Serves 4

You have probably noticed that a number of recipes in this book use pineapple, and I often have half of a pineapple in my fridge. When unexpected visitors drop by, this is an easy, impromptu dessert that I can bust out in less than 15 minutes. If you don't have queso fresco or another crumbly, fresh cheese, use a big spoonful of Greek yogurt instead.

Avocado oil

8 (½-inch) rings fresh pineapple (about ½ large pineapple), peeled and cored

1 cup queso fresco or farmer cheese, crumbled

¼ cup hot honey

Fresh mint leaves, thinly sliced, for garnish

Preheat a ridged grill pan over medium-high heat. Spray or brush with avocado oil.

Arrange the pineapple slices on the pan and grill until they soften and develop nice char marks on both sides, about 8 minutes total.

Arrange two pineapple rings on each serving plate and top with the queso fresco. Drizzle each serving with 1 tablespoon of the hot honey and garnish with a sprinkle of mint.

✳ *Have extra pineapple? Make the Tamarind Soup with Salmon, Tomatoes, and Pineapple on page 128 or the Flash-Fried Flounder with Quick Pineapple Salsa on page 161.*

ROASTED PEACHES *with* BURRATA *and* BALSAMIC DRIZZLE

Serves 4

The flavor and texture of a perfectly ripe peach is a thing of beauty, bursting with juice, soft yet not mushy, a ray of sunshine in every bite. A bad peach, on the other hand, is like biting into a ball of dryer lint—mealy, dry, and devoid of taste. If peaches aren't in season, go ahead and make this with about half of a 16-ounce bag of frozen peach wedges instead. They won't get as nicely browned, but you'll spare yourself a mouthful of disappointment! I find peaches have an affinity for the flavors in Chinese five-spice powder, which I've combined here with sweet balsamic vinegar for an easy but sophisticated dessert. Served on a piece of grilled bread, this would also be an awesome afternoon snack or even an appetizer.

2 large or 4 small peaches, halved

1 tablespoon agave nectar

1 cup balsamic vinegar

¼ teaspoon Chinese five-spice powder

4 small (approximately 1.5-ounce) balls burrata cheese, or one large ball, torn into four pieces

Fresh Thai basil or mint leaves, for garnish

Preheat the oven to 425°F.

Place the peach halves on a rimmed baking sheet lined with foil or parchment paper. Brush the cut surfaces with the agave nectar and roast until the peaches are soft and lightly browned on the edges, about 20 minutes.

While the peaches roast, pour the balsamic vinegar into a small saucepan. Stir in the five-spice powder and bring to a simmer over medium heat. Cook the vinegar at a low boil, adjusting the heat as necessary, until reduced to about ⅓ cup, about 15 minutes.

To assemble, place a peach half (or halves) into each of four dessert bowls. Arrange mozzarella on top of each portion of peaches. Drizzle with the balsamic vinegar syrup, garnish with the basil leaves, and serve.

If you like the flavor that the five-spice powder adds here, try the Sheet-Pan Five-Spice Chicken Legs with Squash and Broccolini on page 167.

ROASTED PEACHES
with BURRATA *and*
BALSAMIC DRIZZLE

page 235

CHOCOLATE HAZELNUT MOUSSE

Serves 6

Elegant enough to serve at a fancy dinner party, this dense, rich pudding provides a lot of chocolate satisfaction in every petite serving. A base of silken tofu gives each bite a secret protein superpower, but it's the über-rich Nutella-on-steroids flavor that will have you licking your spoon. I think this mousse looks really pretty served in espresso cups, which is also a smart way to control the portion size.

1½ cups hazelnuts

1 teaspoon instant espresso powder or 2 teaspoons instant coffee crystals

5 ounces bittersweet chocolate, chopped into small pieces

8 ounces silken tofu, drained

½ cup maple syrup

1 teaspoon vanilla extract

¼ teaspoon kosher salt

½ cup Cashew Crème (page 231) or whipped cream

½ pint fresh raspberries, for garnish

Preheat the oven to 350°F.

Spread the hazelnuts on a rimmed baking sheet and toast until they are fragrant and slightly darker in color, 8 to 10 minutes. Reserve ½ cup of the hazelnuts and place the rest in the bowl of a food processor. Allow the nuts to cool for about 10 minutes.

While the nuts cool, combine the espresso powder in a cup with 1 teaspoon of hot water, stir until smooth, and set aside. Place the chocolate in a microwave-safe bowl and microwave on high in 30-second increments, stirring after each interval. Stop microwaving when a few small pieces of unmelted chocolate still remain; the residual heat will finish melting the chocolate. Stir until smooth.

Process the hazelnuts until they're ground to a paste consistency, about 3 minutes, stopping to scrape down the sides of the bowl once or twice. The smoother the paste is, the nicer the texture of your mousse will be.

Add the tofu, maple syrup, vanilla, espresso, and salt to the hazelnuts, and blend until smooth. Add the chocolate and blend until uniformly colored.

Pour the mousse into 6 espresso cups or small ramekins and chill for at least 1 hour.

To serve, chop the reserved ½ cup of toasted hazelnuts. Top each serving with a small dollop of cashew crème and sprinkle with the chopped nuts and raspberries.

Blend any remaining tofu into The Mocha Protein Smoothie on page 54, or use it to make two servings (or four small ones) of Maple Ginger Tofu (page 228).

BARK BITES *with* QUINOA CRUNCHIES

Makes 12 candies

Elegant and sophisticated, these bittersweet bites have a healthy secret: puffed quinoa. You may have to hunt for these cereal-like quinoa bits (I've tried to make them at home and it just isn't the same), but some natural food stores carry them and they are available online. If you can't find them, no worries—you can substitute hemp hearts or just make them without, but I do enjoy the crunch (and the teensy bit of protein) they add to a dessert that is otherwise straight-up indulgent. Sprinkle with a few goji berries to reinforce the "healthy" vibe.

½ cup puffed quinoa

8 ounces semisweet or bittersweet chocolate (go for the good stuff if you can)

½ cup mixed nuts, seeds, and slivered dried fruit, such as goji berries, dried cherries, dried cranberries, apricots, golden raisins, pistachios, roasted cashews, toasted coconut, etc.

Place a sheet of parchment paper on a rimmed baking sheet and use a pencil to trace twelve 3-inch circles onto the paper, spacing them evenly. Flip the parchment paper pencil-side down and spoon about 2 teaspoons of the quinoa onto each circle, spreading them evenly.

Chop the chocolate into small pieces and place about three-quarters of them in a heatproof glass measuring cup. Microwave on high in 30-second increments, stirring after each interval, until the chocolate is very fluid and hot to the touch, about 2 minutes total. Add the remaining chopped chocolate and stir until melted. Immediately pour the chocolate over the quinoa on the prepared baking sheet, using the penciled circles as a guide and covering all the quinoa. Use a small offset spatula or a spoon to spread the chocolate in an even circle, but don't spread it too thinly.

Before the chocolate sets, decorate the tops of these bites with the nuts, seeds, and fruits. Rap the pan on the counter a few times to settle the toppings into the chocolate, then set aside to let the bites harden completely, at least 1 hour or more, depending on how warm your kitchen is.

When the bites are firm, peel them off the parchment paper and store in an airtight container for up to 2 weeks.

Have extra puffed quinoa? Add it to the Oat Crumble (page 230) or Blue-on-Blue Smoothie Bowl (page 50).

CHOCOLATE SALAMI

Makes two 5-inch logs

I use this sausage look-alike for the centerpiece of my Fresh "Char-fruit-erie" Board (page 217) because it really drives home the cured-meat illusion, but it is a fun little treat in its own right. Serve a few slices with a cup of espresso (it is actually a traditional Italian sweet) or as a gluten-free addition to a cookie tray. The final coating of confectioners' sugar here is the only exception to my no-refined-sugar rule, but you don't need much. You could also swap in oat flour if you are feeling really virtuous! (See photo, page 216.)

4 ounces bittersweet chocolate, cut into small pieces

2 tablespoons unsalted butter

2 tablespoons heavy cream

½ cup almond flour

¼ cup cocoa powder

½ teaspoon kosher salt

½ teaspoon red food coloring (optional)

1 cup raw cashews, coarsely chopped

Confectioners' sugar for rolling

In a small saucepan, combine the chocolate, butter, and cream and stir over low heat until the chocolate has just melted, stirring frequently. Remove from the heat and add the almond flour, cocoa powder, salt, and food coloring (if using); stir to make a thick paste. Scrape the chocolate mixture onto a cutting board and sprinkle with the cashews, then fold and knead until the cashews are incorporated. Form the mixture into a log about 1½ inches in diameter.

Dust a piece of parchment paper with confectioners' sugar and place the log on top. Roll the log back and forth to coat it evenly with the sugar on all sides. Roll up the log in the parchment and twist the ends tightly.

Refrigerate the "salami" for 2 hours, or until it is firm, then slice into ⅓-inch rounds to serve. Wrap any leftovers in plastic and store at room temperature for a week or two.

✻ *Almond flour is on the pricey side and can go rancid quickly, so use any leftover flour to make some Apple Walnut Muffins (page 64), or store it in the freezer.*

241

AMAZING DATES

Makes 12 candies

The first time I popped one of these in my mouth, I couldn't believe how much it tasted like a Snickers bar—and millions of people on Instagram agreed with me! These bites, which combine dates, peanut butter, and chocolate, take just a minute to put together. And because they are made with pantry ingredients you probably already have in the cupboard, once you've got this down, you'll never have to hit the vending machine when you need a little something sweet to end a meal.

12 large soft dates, preferably Medjool
¾ cup smooth peanut butter or other nut butter
12 pecan halves
8 ounces semisweet chocolate chips or bittersweet chocolate chunks
Flaky sea salt

With a sharp paring knife, split the dates lengthwise and remove the pits, keeping the date intact. Fill the cavity with 1 tablespoon of peanut butter and press a pecan half into the peanut butter. Close the date around the filling.

Place the chocolate in a microwave-safe bowl and microwave on high in 20-second increments, stirring after each interval, until melted, about 1 minute total. Stir the chocolate until it is completely smooth. Dip the stuffed dates into the melted chocolate, covering about three-quarters of each date, and place on a sheet of parchment paper. Sprinkle with a bit of salt.

Refrigerate the dates until the chocolate coating has hardened, about 30 minutes, then store in an airtight container at room temperature for a week or two.

❄ *Dates are a great natural sweetener; use one or two in a smoothie or use a handful to make my Spiced Orange Caramel Sauce (page 218), which contains no refined sugar.*

Acknowledgments

There are so many people to thank for their help and guidance in putting together the book you hold in your hands

It's a cliché, I know, but I truly could not have done *any* of this without the support of my family, especially my husband, Harlan, for taking on more at home so I can pursue my career, and daughters, Shay and Keira, who are my best friends and biggest cheerleaders. My parents made sure I never forgot the food of their homeland even when we were getting by on food stamps—and still drop by to fry up a batch of bahn xeo or leave us a platter of meticulously sliced fruit nearly every single day!

I am also indebted to the following:

- My managers, Barbara Jones and Shanna Fischer, helped me navigate my career and pushed me out of my comfort zone.
- David Doerrer was my publishing guide. He landed me in the talented hands of my team at Rodale, led by Diana Baroni, editor Dervla Kelly, and art director Jenny Davis. They were ably assisted by Katherine Leak, Ada Yonenaka, Jonathan Sung, and Kelly Doyle in helping my work make its way into the world.
- Erin Kunkel put together a fun and hardworking team to create the photos for this book, and designer Sebit Min transformed them into the eye-catching and easy-to-use pages you see here.
- My writer, Pam Krauss, saw my vision and brought this book to life with me.

Last, and most important, my deepest gratitude goes to everyone on social media who has encouraged me to keep cooking, creating, and exploring what it meant to be healthy *my* way for nearly twelve years now. From my first tentative post of overnight oats, you have let me know what you liked (and didn't love) and what you wanted to see more of (I hope this book shows I got the message!), and given me the confidence to express myself and my food as authentically as I know how. That so many of you have stuck with me for the whole crazy journey means more to me than you can imagine.

Index

About the Author

MY NGUYEN is the creator behind @MyHealthyDish, a social media empire with more than nine million highly engaged followers. She is a second-generation Vietnamese Californian who grew up in the Vietnamese restaurant her parents owned and ran.

Published in the United States by Rodale Books,
    an imprint of Random House, a division of
    Penguin Random House LLC, New York.
RodaleBooks.com | RandomHouseBooks.com
RODALE and the Plant colophon are registered
    trademarks of Penguin Random House LLC.
Library of Congress Cataloging-in-Publication Data
Names: Nguyen, My, author.
Title: Healthy, my way / My Nguyen.
Description: First edition. | New York : Rodale,
    [2024] | Includes index.
Identifiers: LCCN 2023041829 (print) |
    LCCN 2023041830 (ebook) |
    ISBN 9780593580189 (hardcover) |
    ISBN 9780593580196 (ebook)
Subjects: LCSH: Cooking, Asian. | Cooking
    (Natural foods) | LCGFT: Cookbooks.
Classification: LCC TX724.5.A1 N496 2024
    (print) | LCC TX724.5.A1 (ebook) |
    DDC 641.5/637—dc23/eng/20230927
LC record available at
    https://lccn.loc.gov/2023041829
LC ebook record available at
    https://lccn.loc.gov/2023041830
Printed in China

Book Design by Sebit Min
Food Styling by Erin Quon
    (assistant Cole Church)
Prop Styling by Leila Nichols

10 9 8 7 6 5 4 3 2 1
First Edition